GARDENING
LAB
= = = = = = = =
✳ FOR KIDS ✳

GARDENING LAB

FOR KIDS

52 Fun Experiments to Learn, Grow, Harvest,
Make, Play, and Enjoy Your Garden

Renata Fossen Brown

Quarry Books
100 Cummings Center, Suite 406L
Beverly, MA 01915

quarrybooks.com • craftside.typepad.com

First published in the United States of America in 2014 by
Quarry Books, a member of
Quayside Publishing Group
100 Cummings Center
Suite 406-L
Beverly, Massachusetts 01915-6101
Telephone: (978) 282-9590
Fax: (978) 283-2742
www.quarrybooks.com
Visit www.Craftside.Typepad.com for a behind-the-scenes peek at our crafty world!

10 9 8 7 6 5 4 3 2 1

ISBN: 978-1-59253-904-8

Digital edition published in 2014
eISBN: 978-1-62788-030-5

Library of Congress Cataloging-in-Publication Data
Brown, Renata Fossen.
  Hands on family : gardening lab for kids / Renata Fossen Brown.
      p. cm.
  Gardening lab for kids
  ISBN 978-1-59253-904-8
  1. Gardening for children. 2. Children's gardens. I. Title. II. Title: Gardening lab for kids.
  SB457.B723 2014
  635.083--dc23
                                              2013038945

Design: Leigh Ring // www.ringartdesign.com
Cover Image: Dave Brown
Photography: Dave Brown // www.davebrownimages.com

Printed in China

* DEDICATION *

To my mom and dad. My mom has the greenest thumb in the world, and our home was always filled with thriving, happy houseplants. Thankfully, I inherited a tiny portion of that gene. From my dad the farmer, I always had a garden, always reduced, reused, and recycled and thought everyone composted. I love you both very much, and thank you for the wonderful green values you instilled in me.

* CONTENTS *

* INTRODUCTION *

It's been said that "gardening is better than therapy and you get tomatoes." I would agree. Gardening is also the combination of art and science. This book is a collection of activities I've used both professionally at Cleveland Botanical Garden and personally during the past twenty years. To me, gardening is everything good: exercise (but more fun), being outside (usually), communing with nature, and (hopefully) bettering a tiny patch of earth. I'm not a professional gardener, I'm not a horticulturist, but I do hang out with a bunch of them and ask a lot of questions. The biggest thing I've learned through these interactions is that all of those "rules" they learned in school are simply there to be broken.

Gardening is a personal endeavor, and whatever makes you happy should be what you do. If you love putting pinks and oranges together because they make you smile, then do it. If, instead of the rules of three, you prefer groups of four, then do it.

I get great ideas of things to do in my yard from daily walks with the dogs, plant catalogs, and Pinterest! From these same three places, I also see plenty of things I don't want in my yard. Either way, you learn new things to implement—or not.

UNIT № 01

* GARDEN BASICS *

BENEFITS OF GARDENING

If you are flipping through this book, you already enjoy being around plants, so we don't need to convince you of that. In addition to gardening being a great hobby, there are numerous health benefits to it. Gardening outside is great exercise because there's a lot of walking, squatting, stretching, lifting, and bending involved. All of this movement increases oxygen flow to the muscles and brain and increases a sense of well-being and calm. Working outdoors connects us with nature, which has been shown to work wonders for children having a hard time focusing.

* PLANT PARTS *

A plant has four basic parts: root, stem, leaf, flower. To have healthy plants, you need to know how each part functions.

ROOT: The main jobs of the root are to anchor and absorb. Roots hold a plant in place while absorbing water and nutrients from the soil. Roots grow into the spaces between soil particles, which is why it is important not to have compacted soil. Roots need water, but many plant roots will rot and die if they are in wet soil for a long time.

STEM: A stem also has two jobs: to transport and support. Water and nutrients that were absorbed by the roots are moved through the rest of the plant via the stem. The sugars made in the leaf through the process of photosynthesis are moved back down the stem and throughout the plant via the stem as well. Stems can be vertical, horizontal, underground, or aboveground, and they support the leaves of the plant.

LEAF: The leaf is the most important part of the plant. This is where the process of photosynthesis happens. Water and nutrients combine with carbon dioxide and sunlight in a chemical reaction to create food for the plant in the form of sugar. This sugar fuels all other life on the planet. An animal that eats plants ingests this sugar and is then able to continue on with its day. When another animal eats that animal, the second animal takes in some of that energy and is able to continue on with its day, and so on.

Two excellent by-products of photosynthesis are water and oxygen, our favorite gas. The more leaves there are on the planet, the more carbon dioxide gets absorbed out of the atmosphere and the more oxygen we have to breathe. A win-win if ever there was one.

FLOWER: Besides being a pretty face, flowers are responsible for plant reproduction. When a bee visits a flower looking for nectar to eat, it picks up a little bit of that flower's pollen. It then goes to another flower looking for more nectar, and some of the pollen from the first flower falls off into the second flower. The pollen may travel through the flower, fertilizing it. A fertilized flower may turn into a fruit, which is merely protection for the seeds growing inside of it. The seeds can then be planted and grow into another flower, propagating the species.

* PLANT HARDINESS AND HEAT ZONES *

Gardening is different wherever you are: Cleveland; London; Phoenix; or Alberta, Canada. The main difference can be found looking at a map of the world's hardiness zones.

When shopping for plants, most plant labels list the plant hardiness zone, which indicates how well a plant will survive cold winters. These zones are numbered from north to south starting at 1. If you live in zone 5, you can have plants labeled for zones 1 through 5. You may be able to push it with a plant labeled zone 6 or 7 in your garden if you know your microclimates (see Lab 20). See Resources, page 132, to find more information about U.S. heat zones and international hardiness zones.

* ANNUAL VERSUS PERENNIAL *

Annuals are plants that complete their life cycle in one year and are typically replaced yearly. In the Midwest, annuals include marigolds, zinnias, petunias, and impatiens. Many of the food crops we think of are also annuals. Annuals are typically used for bold splashes of long-lasting color and ease of maintenance, but can be costly to replace year in and year out.

Perennials are plants that live more than two years. Typically, when using the term *perennial*, people are not referring to shrubs or trees, which also usually live more than two years. Rather, they are talking about plants such as purple coneflower or hosta. Many perennials continue to grow throughout their lifetimes and therefore need to be divided. Each type of plant has preferred methods and times to do this, so you should research before ripping any of your plants apart. Once you do find out though, dividing is a great way to increase the amount of plants in your garden or to give away to friends and neighbors.

* WATERING *

Established plants in a Midwestern garden typically need about one inch of water each week. If Mother Nature isn't providing this (see Lab 9), then you have to. The best time to water your garden is first thing in the morning. When watering, direct the flow of water to the base of the plant, avoiding the leaves as much as possible. Remember, it is the roots that are responsible for water uptake, not the leaves. If leaves are constantly wet, this can cause mildew or other diseases to grow. Not to mention that you will use less water if aiming just at the roots.

* HOW TO PLANT *

If purchasing plants in plastic pots or containers, give them a little love before plunking them in the ground. Dig the hole bigger than the pot the plant came in and scrape up the sides of the hole. This will help the roots grow away from the plant. Carefully remove the plant from the container; sometimes this necessitates cutting the container away from the plant. Once the plant is removed, pull the roots apart gently so that they aren't wrapping around themselves. This encourages healthy growth of the plant. Gently place the plant in the center of the hole and push the soil back around it. Press the soil down firmly (but don't stand on it) so that you remove big air pockets. Water plants well after planting and continue giving additional water throughout the first season if need be.

* GARDENING WITH PETS *

Our pets are members of the family, so be aware of things in your yard for the safety and enjoyment of our four-legged friends. Many plants that are safe for humans can be slightly to extremely toxic to dogs and cats. Crab apples, yews, begonias, coleus, and mums are just a small handful of very common plants to be mindful of around pets. I've had all of these plants in my yard, however, and the dogs have never touched them, but always keep an eye on your animals while in the yard to make sure they aren't ingesting things that may make them sick (or worse). Your veterinarian or poison control center can provide you with a list, as well as the ASPCA (see Resources).

When planting gardens where dogs roam, it's best not to fight nature. Watch where your dog typically walks (usually it is hugging the property perimeter, up against a fence) and DON'T PLANT THERE. Why spend the time, money, and effort of planting a gorgeous plant when odds are Fido is going to run right over it?

* MATERIALS *

The great thing about gardening is you can just go do it without investing money into equipment.

CLOTHES: Throw on some that you don't mind getting dirty. I judge a good day in the garden by how muddy my pants, hands, and hair are!

SHOES: I swear by my rubber garden clogs. Slip them on, get to gardening, and hose them off at the end of the day. Sandals and flip-flops aren't safe (those little toes are exposed) and allow so much dirt into them you'll spend half a day scrubbing your feet when you're done.

GLOVES: A nice tight fit makes gripping things easier. I'm a fan of West County Gloves. Those one-dollar work gloves in the discount bins are always too big and quite useless. Invest in a good fitting pair, and they'll last forever.

WATER CONTAINER: Stay hydrated when gardening outside! Use a bottle with a lid to keep stray soil, bugs, and leaves out.

TROWEL: This is a small, hand-held shovel that you'll use all the time. Don't waste your time with a cheap plastic one. You'll break it soon enough. Invest in a metal one with a pointed tip (not rounded) and sturdy construction. Test it in the store and try to bend it where the handle meets the blade. I've got a groovy ergonomic one from Radius Garden that is fantastic.

Honestly, that's all you need.

UNIT №02

* GETTING STARTED *

Sometimes people get a little uptight about gardening. They believe there are "rules!" and you have to do it "right!" But this is all simply a bunch of nonsense. Gardening should make you happy, and you should follow your instincts. How unfortunate it would be to go through the work of gardening just to wind up with a bunch of plants you don't like, in colors that make you queasy, just because you were following someone else's ideas on "proper gardening"? Ick.

These first few labs will teach you different techniques and concepts, but remember that you can change things up to suit your tastes. These are good labs to do as you begin gardening for the first time so that you can grow the biggest and best plants on your street. These activities are just a small sampling of information though; entire books are written just on garden design, for example, and we are doing just a couple activities on it. But you'll get the idea and be able to then experiment, creating your own unique garden spaces.

* MATERIALS *

→ Sandwich-size resealable plastic bag

→ Paper towel

→ Stapler and staples

→ Water

→ 4 lima bean seeds soaked in water for a couple of hours

Gardening begins with seeds, and seeds are magical. These tiny, hard, seemingly inert pieces of nature contain all of the energy and genetic information to grow a carrot, a flower, or a 200-foot (61 m) redwood tree. They are amazing and fun to watch grow!

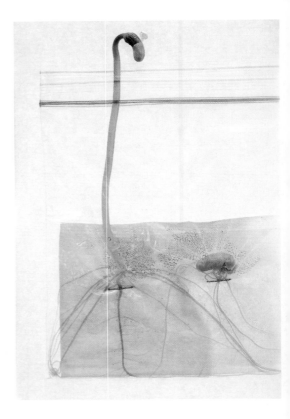

Fig. 1: Fold and put the paper towel in the bag.

* DIG IN! *

1. Fold the paper towel so that it fits along the entire bottom of the bag, and is about 3" (8 cm) high. (Fig. 1)

2. Put a line of three staples across the bag, through both layers of the bag and the paper towel (about 1" [2.5 cm] below the top of the paper towel). (Fig. 2)

Fig. 2: Add three staples.

Fig. 3: Wet and wring out the paper towel.

Fig. 4: Add beans to the bag.

3. Add water to the bag, completely wetting the paper towel. Squeeze out all excess water; too much moisture will cause the seeds to rot. (Fig. 3)

4. Place one bean seed on top of each staple and seal up the bag. You will have one seed left over (see "Dig Deeper!" below). (Fig. 4)

5. Keep the bag in a warm location (taping it to a sunny window works well). At first, seeds do not need sunlight, but once the plants have leaves, they need it to make food. This type of seed germinates (sprouts) very quickly and within ten days will grow out of the bag! (See image on page 20.)

✳ DIG DEEPER! ✳
EXPLORE THE SEED COAT AND ENDOSPERM

→ If you are doing this project in the spring, once the bean plants have sprouted and grown out of the plastic bag, you can gently remove and plant them outside. Wet the paper towel thoroughly first. Be very careful pulling the roots off of the paper towel, making sure that the roots remain intact.

→ Take a look at the bean seed that is left over. After soaking the seeds, you probably noticed that instead of the outside being smooth and hard, it has become softer and bumpy. This outside covering is the seed coat (also called the testa), and just like a coat protects people from the weather, the seed coat protects the inside of the seed from water, pests, and other injury.

→ Inside the seed coat is the energy the plant uses to begin growth before it can photosynthesize (or make its own food). This is called the endosperm. If you carefully peel off the seed coat from the leftover fourth bean and open the seed into two pieces, you should see a tiny plant, called the embryo, at the base of the seed.

* MATERIALS *

→ Garden hose

→ Spray paint (optional)

→ Straight-edged shovel

Creating the shape and size of your garden can be simple ("a perfect square!") or not ("curves, circles, loops, oh my!"). When planning the size, you need to consider how much work you will put into maintaining the garden (large gardens can be a large amount of work) and how you will access the center of the garden. When planning the shape, keep in mind if a lawn mower needs to move alongside it and if it can make those turns.

Before you start digging up the sod or planting your plants, it's good to try out several different shapes and sizes using this simple method to see what you like best.

Fig. 1: Try different potential shapes.

* DIG IN! *

1. Unroll the garden hose into a shape you may like for your garden. (Fig. 1)

2. Can you reach into the center of the garden? Can a lawn mower move around the edges easily? (Fig. 2)

3. Move the hose around, creating different shapes and sizes until you are satisfied. If desired, use the spray paint to mark the size and shape of the garden. (Fig. 3)

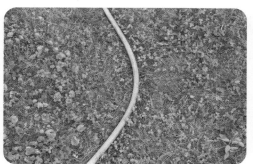

Fig. 2: Make sure a lawn mower can handle your garden's curves.

Fig. 3: Spray paint the shape.

Fig. 4: Dig into the edge of your garden.

4. Place the shovel against the outside edge of the hose and press it into the ground. If you are removing grass, push the shovel down at least 4" (10 cm). Continue this around the entire perimeter of your garden. (Fig. 4)

✳ DIG DEEPER! ✳

HOW MUCH SUN DOES YOUR GARDEN GET?

If nothing is shading your garden (such as a tree, house, or fence), your garden is going to receive "full sun" all day. But most likely, something will be shading your plants at some point during the day. When selecting plants, choose between plants requiring "full sun" (receiving six or more hours of direct sunlight a day), "full shade" (receiving less than three hours of direct sunlight a day), "partial sun" (three to six hours of direct sunlight a day), and "partial shade" (two to four hours of direct sunlight a day).

* MATERIALS *

→ Soil thermometer

→ Shovel or hoe

→ Metal bow rake

→ 2' to 3' (61 to 91 cm) metal or wooden straight edge

→ Seeds: lettuce, spinach, and radish

Once the ground has warmed in early spring, you can plant "cool season" crops. These are plants that do best in cooler weather and can even withstand mild frosts. Plant some of the same types of seeds one week apart so you get a staggered harvest, and you aren't inundated with all of your radishes, for example, all at once. Before starting, make sure the soil is not too wet. Take a handful and press it into your hand. If it stays in a ball it's too wet. If it crumbles apart it's perfect!

* DIG IN! *

1. Push the soil thermometer into the soil in your selected location. For early spring crops, a temperature of 42°F (5.5°C) is necessary. If the soil temperature is 42°F (5.5°C) or a little bit above, you are ready to plant! (Fig. 1)

2. Loosen the soil and break up any big clumps using a shovel or hoe. Then smooth the surface with a metal bow rake. (Fig. 2)

3. These seeds only need to be planted ¼" to ½" (6.35 to 12.7 mm) below the surface, so use a straight piece of metal or wood to make an even furrow in the soil. Lay it on top of the soil and gently press down to the proper depth. (Fig. 3)

4. Lay your seeds in the furrow the distance apart indicated on your seed packet, then cover carefully with soil. (Fig. 4)

Fig. 1: Check the soil temperature.

Fig. 2: Prepare the soil.

Fig. 3: Create an even furrow in the soil.

Fig. 4: Plant the seeds $1/4$" to $1/2$" (6.35 to 12.7 mm) apart.

5. Water your seeds gently, as shown on page 24, using the mist option on a hose or a spray bottle. You don't want to dislodge your carefully planted seeds with a giant blast of water! Seeds need to stay moist, so watering daily until they sprout may be necessary. Seedlings can go just a bit longer between waterings, but will also need to be checked on daily for their watering needs. Keep an eye on your seeds to germinate (to begin to sprout and grow); you'll be able to eat your radishes in about three weeks and your lettuce and spinach in six to seven weeks! Yummo!

✳ DIG DEEPER! ✳
WHAT ARE HEIRLOOM SEEDS?

→ Have you ever heard of heirloom seeds? When you hear the word *heirloom*, you may think of anything worth saving, such as antiques or grandma's china plates, or your great-great-great uncle's favorite lamp. It's something that gets passed on to the next generation. Heirloom seeds are along the same lines; they are worth saving and passing on for the next season.

→ Many of the seeds you'll see for sale at garden centers and other stores are hybrids, meaning two different plants were selected for certain qualities and hand-pollinated. If you collect hybrid seeds at the end of the season, they probably won't grow (they may be sterile), or if they do grow, the plants might not look like the original plant you put in the ground. Heirloom seeds, however, will grow true to form and are usually very dependable and hardy. Many times, heirloom vegetables have been selected because of their fuller flavor.

* MATERIALS *

→ Permanent marker

→ Cardboard egg earton

→ Seed-starting mix

→ Spoon or small trowel

→ Seeds: tomato, hot pepper, sweet pepper, and so on

→ Spray bottle

Starting seedlings indoors is an easy way to save money because a packet of seeds is much cheaper than a tray full of plants. It's also a great way to start gardening earlier in the season rather than having to wait until it warms up outside. Before starting this Lab, cover your workspace with newspapers and gather your materials.

Fig. 1: Fill each segment with soil.

* DIG IN! *

1. Use a permanent marker to label the lid of the egg carton with the names of the seeds you will plant in each segment. Using a spoon or small trowel, fill each indentation with soil. (Fig. 1)

2. Plant your seeds to the proper depth (read the package directions for each type of seed). (Fig. 2)

3. Use your spray bottle to water your seeds. A spray bottle, as opposed to a watering can, lightly waters your seeds so they don't wash away. (Fig. 3)

Fig. 2: Plant your seeds.

Fig. 3: Gently water your seeds.

Fig. 4: Keep the seeds warm and check daily for growth.

4. Close the lid on your container and put it somewhere warm. Check your seeds daily. Once plants begin to pop through the soil, keep the lid open and make sure your seeds get plenty of light. If using an artificial light, keep your seedlings 1" to 2" (2.5 to 7.5 cm) from the light. When your seedlings are ready to transplant outside, cut the egg carton sections apart. Based on the seed package directions, plant your seedlings (egg carton section and all) in the ground at the directed distance apart from each other. Water your plants in well. (Fig. 4)

✳ DIG DEEPER! ✳
START SEEDLINGS INDOORS

→ Once seeds sprout, use a ruler to measure your plants every morning. Create a chart to keep track of how much they grow every day. You'll be surprised how fast some seedlings grow!

Plant seeds indoors six to ten weeks before your last frost date. You can look up this information online or in gardening books. Every area's frost date is different, so look up your own. At www.plantmaps.com, you can enter your ZIP code to find the last date in the spring your area typically gets frost.

→ As your seedlings get taller, lower them from the light source so that the tops of your plants still remain 1" to 2" (2.5 to 5 cm) below it. If your light source can be raised higher, do that; if not, place your egg carton on books or cans that you can remove gradually to lower the plants away from the light.

* MATERIALS *

→ Wooden crate

→ Ruler

→ Paint brush

→ Drill and drill bit

→ Exterior paint

→ ⅝" (16 mm) braided polyester rope

One of the many good things about gardening is that you can accomplish everything with just a few good tools. Of course, you can go crazy and accumulate every tool in the world, but you really only need a couple. While going about your work, it's handy to have a tote to store and carry them around the yard in. Here's one you can personalize as much as you want.

* DIG IN! *

1. On the sides of the wooden crate, measure 1" (2.5 cm) from the top. Then measure where the midpoint is horizontally and mark it. (Fig. 1)

2. With adult assistance, use a drill to make a hole on each side of the crate for the rope, which will become your handle. (Fig. 2)

3. Get creative and paint up your tote! Allow it to dry. (Fig. 3)

4. From the outside of the crate, thread the rope through each hole and knot each end tightly. (Fig. 4)

5. Proudly put your garden tools inside for storing and carrying.

Fig. 1: Measure the midpoint.

Fig. 2: Drill a hole in each side of the crate.

Fig. 3: Paint your tote.

Fig. 4: Push the rope through each hole and knot.

✳ DIG DEEPER! ✳

CARING FOR GARDEN TOOLS

→ Take care of your tools! When you are done gardening each day, clean off and dry your tools to prevent them from rusting.

→ At the end of each growing season, after you've "put your garden to bed," you should also put your tools to bed for the winter. For shovels, pitchforks, hoes, and trowels, sand the wood handles with sandpaper to smooth any rough edges, then oil the wood with linseed oil. You can find linseed oil at hardware stores. Clean the metal blades with water and a wire brush and dry thoroughly. Use a small amount of linseed oil on the blade to prevent rusting.

→ For pruners and loppers, clean and dry them after each use. At the end of the season, take them apart, lubricate all edges with linseed oil, and store them in a dry place. When needed, use a metal file to sharpen the blades.

→ Disconnect hoses from the house and straighten them out. Beginning at one end, lift the hose over your head to get the water flowing out the other end. Slowly start gathering up the hose in a loop around your arm. Don't go too fast or you'll wind up with water left inside the hose that could freeze and weaken or break the hose.

* MATERIALS *

→ Plant or seed catalogs with color pictures

→ Rough outline sketch of your garden

→ Scissors

→ Glue

Fig. 1: Cut out pictures of plants.

Before you put your plants in the ground, decide where they will go in your garden without even getting dirty. This Lab is also a simple way of seeing which colors and textures you like next to each other. Before beginning, clear a space to work on a table and lay down newspapers.

 *** DIG IN! ***

1. Cut out pictures of plants you like. Write the plant names on your garden sketch or in your garden journal (Lab 42) and note how tall each gets. (Fig. 1)

2. Arrange the pictures in your garden sketch. Place taller plants behind smaller plants so they won't be hiding or shading them. (Fig. 2)

Fig. 2: Arrange the plant pictures.

Fig. 3: Glue the pictures in place.

Fig. 4: Your completed design.

3. Once you are pleased with their positions, glue the pictures in place. (Fig. 3)

4. You can use your completed masterpiece as a guideline on planting a real garden, or hang it somewhere to admire. (Fig. 4)

||||||||||||||||||||||||||||||||||||||||||||||| * **DIG DEEPER!** * |||||||||||||||||||||||||||||||||||||||||||||||

TIPS FOR DESIGNING YOUR GARDEN

When designing a garden, people usually plant things in groups of three or five or some other odd number. This doesn't have to be three of the same plant; this can be three different plants of the same color placed throughout your garden. For example, if you've chosen one black-eyed Susan (yellow petals), you may want to then choose two yellow yarrow plants for elsewhere in your garden so you'd have a total of three yellow plants. Odd numbers of plants are used because we typically like odd numbers of things—but remember, do what you like!

→ One thing to keep in mind is that even if you love one color and only want your garden to have that color leaves or petals in it, you should incorporate other, contrasting-color plants in your garden. This helps your favorite colors "pop," or stand out, against the other colors.

* MATERIALS *

→ Toilet paper

→ Ruler

→ Pen or marker

→ 1 tablespoon (7.8 g) flour

→ Water

→ Cotton swab

→ Packet of seeds

Fig. 1: Measure and mark the distance the seeds will be planted.

You could spend millions of dollars buying premade seed tape from a nursery (ok, more like five dollars), or you can make your very own for about ten cents with things you already have in the house. You decide. Regardless, this is an effective way of planting seeds at the right spacing, especially when the seeds are very small.

* DIG IN! *

1. Unroll the toilet paper on your work surface to the length of the area in which you will plant it. Use the ruler to measure the distance the seeds should be planted apart from each other and mark that on the toilet paper with the pen or marker. (Fig. 1)

2. Mix the flour with a little bit of water to create a gooey paste. This is how you will adhere the seeds to the tape. Make sure the paste isn't watery—you want it as dry as possible while still being able to stick the seeds to the paper. (Fig. 2)

Fig. 2: Create a paste to adhere the seeds to the paper.

Fig. 3: Apply the paste to the paper.

Fig 4: Place the seeds into each mound of paste.

3. Dip the cotton swab into the paste, then dab the paste onto the first few marks on the toilet paper. Don't put paste on all of the marks at once; you don't want the paste to dry before you put on the seeds. (Fig. 3)

4. Carefully place one to two seeds on each glob of paste so that they stick. (Fig. 4)

5. Repeat steps 3 and 4 until you've completed the length of toilet paper, then allow the paper to dry. When it is ready, plant the length of seed tape at the required depth and water it well. (Fig. 5)

Fig. 5: Plant your seed tape.

DIG DEEPER!

SEED TAPE MAKES A GREAT GIFT

→ Seed tape can be a great gift for your favorite gardener. Prepare several with different kinds of seeds and roll them up when they are dry. Put them in plastic bags and keep in the refrigerator until you are ready to give them. Write on each bag the name of the seed and how deep the tape should be planted.

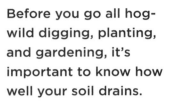

* MATERIALS *

→ Shovel

→ Hose or bucket full of water

→ Ruler

→ Timer

Before you go all hog-wild digging, planting, and gardening, it's important to know how well your soil drains. Most plants prefer well-draining soil, but some can be planted in claylike soils, and some do well in sandier soils. This simple activity will help you learn what's going on under your feet.

Fig. 1: Dig a hole.

* DIG IN! *

1. Dig a hole 1' (30 cm) deep and 6" (15 cm) wide. (Fig. 1)

2. Fill the hole with water and let it completely drain out. (Fig. 2)

3. Place the ruler in the hole. Fill the hole again, note the measurement on the ruler and begin timing. Write down the water level every minute. (Fig. 3)

4. Once the hole is completely drained, note how long it took.

   • 0 to 10 minutes: You have fast draining soil. This may be a good place to plant herbs if it gets a lot of sun.

   • 11 to 60 minutes: You have well-draining soil. This is ideal for the widest range of plant growth.

   • 60+ minutes: You have slow draining soil, which may contain a lot of clay. You may need to amend the soil with compost and/or sand.

Fig. 2: Fill hole with water and let it drain.

Fig. 3: Place the ruler in the hole.

* DIG DEEPER! *

UNDERSTANDING SAND, SILT, AND CLAY

There are three basic elements of soil: sand, silt, and clay. Each of these particles is a different size, and different soils contain various amounts of each of them, in addition to gravel. Here is a way to remember how big each particle is:

→ To be a particle of sand, stand with your arms and legs outstretched as far as possible. Water can easily move between the particles.

→ To be a particle of silt, stand with hands on your hips and feet closer together. Water could still move between these two particles, but it's a bit more difficult.

→ To be a particle of clay, keep your arms down at your sides and your feet together. It would be very difficult for water to get between these two particles of clay.

Two particles of sand.

Two particles of silt.

Two particles of clay.

* MATERIALS *

→ Plastic, straight-sided water or soda bottle

→ Scissors

→ Ruler

→ Tape

→ Permanent marker

→ Coat hanger

It's important to know how much rain falls in your garden so you know how much you need to water your plants. Typically, gardens only need about 1" (2.5 cm) of water per week, but that depends on whether you have newly planted plants or your garden receives full sun all day. Regardless, it's good to know!

Fig. 1: Pinch and cut the bottle.

* DIG IN! *

1. Pinch the bottle together near its "shoulders" so you have an area to start cutting. Cut into that pinched area with your scissors to form an opening that you can then fit your scissors into to cut all the way around the bottle. (Fig. 1)

2. Lightly tape the ruler to the outside of the bottle (you will remove the ruler shortly). Using the marker, mark 1" (2.5 cm) segments on the bottle and number them. (Fig. 2)

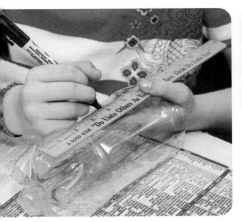

Fig. 2: Mark the bottle.

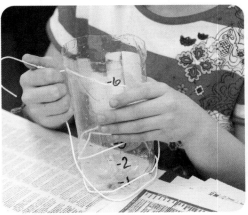

Fig. 3: Twist the coat hanger into loops.

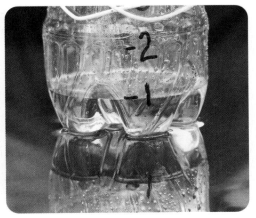

Fig. 4: Measure and document the rainfall.

3. To make a holder for the bottle, bend the bottom part of the coat hanger into three loops that stack on top of each other and fit the bottle inside. (Fig. 3)

4. Use the hook part of the hanger to attach your rain gauge to a fence or other structure outside. Make sure nothing is above this area that could block rainfall, such as a tree or garage overhang. Measure the rain. Be sure to record the amount of rain and empty the gauge after each rainfall. (Fig. 4)

* DIG DEEPER! *

MEASURING RAINFALL FOR YOUR GARDEN

Because every soda or water bottle is different, this isn't a precise way of measuring rainfall. To accurately measure it, you would use math skills to find the surface area and diameter of the container and then measure rainfall in milliliters. Making the gauge as instructed above, however, does give you an accurate way to compare rainfall from one week to the next. You will record this information in your garden journal (Lab 42).

→ The rainiest place on earth is Mount Waialeale in Kauai, Hawaii, averaging over 450" (1143 cm) of rain yearly.

→ Typical vegetable gardens need 1" (2.5 cm) of rain weekly.

MATERIALS

→ Empty plastic soda bottle with cap

→ Scratch awl

→ 1 outlet end hose connector with water stop

→ 1 faucet adapter

→ Hose with water connection

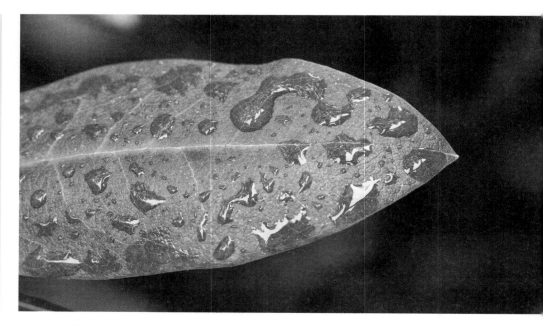

During the hottest summer days, extra watering may be necessary in your garden. If your rain barrel (Lab 25) is empty, it may be time to resort to using the hose. But why not use a sprinkler that you make while keeping materials out of the landfill?

* DIG IN! *

1. With the cap on the bottle, use the scratch awl to poke small holes all over three sides of the bottle. Leave one side of the bottle intact so you aren't just watering the ground below it. (Fig. 1)

Fig. 1: Poke holes in three sides.

Fig. 2: Connect the adapters.

Fig 3: Use your new sprinkler!

2. Connect the adapters to the bottle. (Fig. 2)

3. Connect the hose to the sprinkler and position the sprinkler near plants that need watering. Monitor the sprinkler and move it near other plants after 15 to 20 minutes. (Fig. 3)

✴ DIG DEEPER! ✴

THE EARLY BIRD CATCHES THE WORM

→ "Where'd all these birds come from?" Birds that eat worms usually start gathering when they notice a sprinkler on. The water hits the ground and starts percolating down through the soil, filling up the air spaces. These air spaces are the same ones worms use to breathe. When worms start running out of air, they head toward the surface, where they are met by a fine, feathered friend interested in lunch.

→ Have you heard of the "dog days of summer?" These are typically the hottest days in the Northern Hemisphere, early July to early August. This is also the time when the Dog Star, Sirius, is in alignment with the sun.

→ Using a sprinkler is one way to water your garden, although not the most environmentally friendly one. A soaker hose uses much less water and directs water right at the base of plants, near the roots.

* MATERIALS *

→ Sapling

→ Shovel

→ One bag humus (about 1 cubic foot)

→ One bag compost (about 1 cubic foot)

→ Hose connected to the water supply

TIP: Healthy trees have shiny, rigid leaves with no holes or other signs of bugs, and there are no injuries to the trunk or bark. If you can see the roots, they are long, and not wrapped around the inside of the container excessively. Smell the roots; they should smell pleasantly earthy and not rotten or stinky.

Some people say, "The best time to plant a tree was twenty years ago. The next best time is today." I love this. And I love planting trees. There is something so hopeful and good about it—you trust that this beautiful creature will grow big and strong and provide a habitat for all sorts of wildlife and beautify the area. It will provide you with shade in the summer and lovely color in the fall, and it will give the squirrels something to run up and down on all spring.

In addition to the environmental reasons to plant trees, there are strong economic ones: You can increase the value of your home by several thousands of dollars; trees provide protection from winter winds if planted on the correct side of your house, keeping your home a bit warmer and potentially decreasing your heating bill; and the shade from trees can decrease your air conditioning costs substantially in the summer. What are you waiting for?

 * DIG IN! *

1. Choose a healthy tree from a reputable nursery. Make sure the roots, trunk, and leaves are free of injury and disease. (Fig. 1)

2. In the desired location, dig a hole as deep as the tree's root ball, and three to four time as wide. Slope the sides to allow for proper root growth, and roughen the sides of the hole to provide an easier path for the roots. (Fig. 2)

3. Gently remove the tree from the container. You may need to lay the tree on its side to do this. Don't pull too hard on the trunk to remove it from the container. You may need to cut the container off; if so, have an adult do this for you. (Fig. 3)

Fig. 1: Check the selected tree is healthy.

Fig. 2: Dig the hole.

Fig. 3: Remove the tree.

Fig. 4: Center the tree.

4. Center the tree in the hole, positioning the root flare (the base of the trunk that begins to widen out to the roots) at ground level. You may need to pile a bit of the soil in the center of the hole to provide a base for the tree to sit on to allow the root flare to remain at ground level. (Fig. 4)

5. Refill the hole with a mixture of soil you dug out, plus the bags of humus and compost. Firmly press the soil down over the roots to prevent big air pockets. (Fig. 5)

6. Place the hose at the edge of the hole, turn the water on low, and water well. It's hard to overwater a newly planted tree, so plan on watering it weekly unless you regularly receive many inches (cm) of rain each week. (Fig. 6)

Fig. 5: Refill the hole.

Fig. 6: Water your tree weekly.

✳ DIG DEEPER! ✳

DON'T "VOLCANO" YOUR MULCH

→ Who knows when it was inaccurately decided that the way to mulch around trees was to mound it right up against the trunk? This is one of the quickest ways to kill a tree. Mulching like this keeps moisture right up against the trunk, fostering fungal diseases and can cause the roots to suffocate, so they start traveling upward, into the mulch to get air and water. When the mulch dries out, those roots dry out, too.

→ Optimal mulching around a newly planted tree is approximately 2" to 3" (5 to 7.6 cm) deep, and only extends out to the tree's dripline: this is the area of ground directly below where rainwater would drip straight down off of the branches.

UNIT № 03

* THEME GARDENING *

Theme gardening is a creative way of designing a garden so that everything in it is related to the chosen theme. You've seen this type of garden when you look at a vegetable garden: every plant in it grows vegetables. You can decide any kind of theme: a color, a type of plant, a geographical location, plants with weird names—anything! In addition to the specific themes we'll show you in this book, here are just a few ideas of other types of theme gardens you could try. Can you think of others?

→ Shade garden (plants that only grow in the shade)

→ Yellow garden (every plant has yellow leaves or flowers)

→ "D" garden (every plant begins with the letter *D*)

→ Kitchen garden (all plants are used in cooking)

→ Magical garden (all plants were once thought to have magical qualities—doesn't that sound fun?)

* MATERIALS *

→ A sunny location

→ Butterfly guidebook or reputable butterfly website

→ Host and nectar plants

→ Trowel

→ Small clay saucer

→ Handful of sand

Butterflies have a pretty cool life cycle, and each kind of butterfly needs particular plants to live. To successfully encourage butterflies to hang out in your garden, you should provide both plants from which butterflies can get nectar and plants their caterpillars can eat. You should also be okay with the fact that a successful butterfly garden will have hungry caterpillars completely eating some of your plants!

Fig. 1: Research the butterflies.

* DIG IN! *

1. Using field guides or the Internet, research to select the types of butterflies you want to attract to your garden. Select butterflies commonly found in your area. Make a list with three columns: List the names of the butterflies in the first column, the host plants of each in the second column, and the nectar plants in the third. (Fig. 1)

2. Circle the common plants. This is now the plant list for your butterfly garden. See if friends and neighbors have any that you can have, or go shopping! (Fig. 2)

3. Plant your butterfly garden in a place with a lot of sun that is sheltered from wind. The south side of a building works well. (Fig. 3)

4. Place the clay saucer in the garden, add some sand and salt to it, and fill it with water. Butterflies need water, too, and this provides a good place for them to "puddle" and may attract more to your garden. (Fig. 4)

Fig. 2: Find the plants on your list that will attract butterflies.

Fig. 3: Plant your butterfly garden.

Fig. 4: Place a saucer in the garden to attract butterflies.

✱ DIG DEEPER! ✱
BUTTERFLY FACTS

Each type of butterfly needs its own specific group of plants from which to get nectar. For example, the Eastern Tiger Swallowtail butterfly likes blue cardinal flower (among others), whereas the Black Swallowtail butterfly ignores blue cardinal flower and heads to joe-pye weed (among other plants).

→ When a butterfly is ready to lay eggs, it starts looking for different plants, referred to as host plants. Using the same two species, Eastern Tiger Swallowtails look for different types of trees, whereas the Black Swallowtail needs different types of herbs, such as dill or parsley.

→ The reason butterflies need to seek out specific plants on which to lay their eggs is because as soon as the caterpillars hatch out of them, they need to start eating. Each type of caterpillar only eats certain types of plants. If a butterfly lays its eggs on the wrong type of plant and the caterpillars hatch out, they won't have anything to eat and will die.

* MATERIALS *

→ Super-small natural materials, such as tiny pine cones, shells, tiny sticks, thin pieces of tree bark, small leaves, small nuts and acorns, and pine needles.

→ Weather-resistant silicone, or indoor/outdoor fast-setting wood glue.

→ Trowel

→ Small plants, such as *Sagina, Asperula*, mosses, *Arenaria, Ageratum, Lobularia*, or miniature ferns. In addition to small plants, look for plants with tiny flowers. If you want to use shrubs or bushes, you can find small dwarf varieties that will work well.

→ Miniature knick-knacks or trinkets, such as furniture, animals, and tools.

Fairies are tiny creatures who live in our gardens and keep an eye on things. You are going to create a beautiful place for your garden fairy to live! Gather your materials and find a small, tucked-away place in your garden to build your fairy garden. This can be an area that is "hidden" so only you and the fairy know where it is, or it can be easy for anyone to see.

* DIG IN! *

1. Choose the location of the fairy house near the back of your chosen space. Clear a small area—a 1' (30 cm) square space is perfect. You don't want to make it too big. Smooth the soil in the location the house will go. (Fig. 1)

Fig. 1: Select and clear an area.

Fig. 2: Build your fairy house.

Fig. 3: Plant and water the plants.

2. Construct the house using the natural materials. Build the frame of the house using the tree bark or something else as sturdy. Glue the pieces together using the silicone or wood glue. Clamp the pieces together if necessary and let dry. (Fig. 2)

3. Place the plants where you think they should go and plant them in the soil. Water them at their roots. Add knick-knacks or trinkets. Step back and admire your new creation. Fairies will be moving in there soon! (Fig. 3)

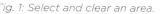

✳ DIG DEEPER! ✳

ATTRACT FAIRIES TO YOUR GARDEN

→ To entice the finest fairy to move into your new house, do some research on plants and herbs that symbolize positive things, such as basil (good wishes), thyme (courage), or sage (wisdom). You can either plant these or scatter some of those leaves around the fairy house!

→ Collect materials for your fairy house by going on a scavenger hunt. Go for a hike in the woods and see what treasures you can find!

* MATERIALS *

→ 1 outdoor round planter, approximately 14" (36 cm) tall and 18" (46 cm) wide at the top

→ Potting soil (enough to fill the selected planter)

→ 3 to 4 tall annual plants with flowers in your favorite sports team's colors

→ Duct tape or other heavy-duty tape

→ Bat and ball, preferably plastic

→ Thin dowel rod, 3' (91 cm) long

→ Silicone adhesive

→ Permanent adhesive letters

Combining gardening and sports? Sure, why not? Here's a fun way to celebrate your favorite sports team.

|||||| * DIG IN! * ||||||

1. Fill the container about ¾ to the top with soil and arrange the plants to fit in the container. Remove the annuals from their pots, plant them into the soil, and water them well. (Fig. 1)

2. Use the duct tape to attach the bat to the dowel rod. Wrap the tape around the smallest part of the bat, where you would be holding it when taking a swing at a fast ball. (Fig. 2)

3. Use the silicone to attach the ball to the bat. Let the silicone dry overnight. (Fig. 3)

4. In your team's colors, use the adhesive letters to spell the words *Go Team!* on the side of the plant container. Place the bat and ball display in the planter, near the back. (Fig. 4)

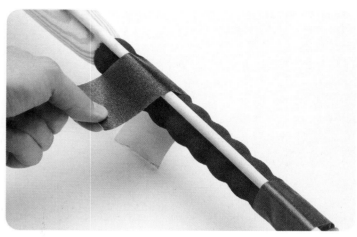

Fig. 1: Plant the annuals and water them.

Fig. 2: Tape the bat to the dowel rod.

Fig. 3: Glue the ball to the bat.

Fig. 4: Spell out "Go Team!" on the container.

* DIG DEEPER! *

TEAM SPIRIT

→ Create other sports-inspired planters in your school colors or a favorite university's colors.

* MATERIALS *

→ Lots of old shoes that will hold soil (high top sneakers and boots are perfect)

→ Scratch awl

→ Soil

→ Assorted annuals

Anything that will hold soil is fair game to plant in. Reusing old shoes is a great way to recycle and be creative.

* DIG IN! *

1. Poke drainage holes in the bottom of each shoe using the awl. You only need three to four depending on the size of the shoe. (Fig. 1)

2. Fill each shoe with soil, leaving room for your annuals. (Fig. 2)

3. Remove each plant from the tray, and gently pull the roots apart to promote plant growth (see page 16). Nestle the plant into the soil and firmly press it into the shoe. Add soil around the roots. Water them each well. Arrange your shoe garden somewhere the whole neighborhood will see it! (Fig. 3)

Fig. 1: Poke drainage holes in the shoes.

Fig. 2: Add soil to each shoe.

Fig. 3: Fill your shoe planters.

✳ DIG DEEPER! ✳
THINK OUTSIDE THE WINDOW BOX

→ The best place in the world to get inspired for your shoe garden is at Cleveland Botanical Garden's Hershey Children's Garden. In this magical gem of a place is the Scrounger's Garden, so named because of the found items used as planting containers. At any time, you may see a filing cabinet filled with pansies, a toilet overflowing with geraniums, a utility sink filled with candytuft, or a purse holding some marigolds. It's the ultimate in reusing and recycling and a great place to inspire you to plant in other things that may be just lying around the house.

* MATERIALS *

→ Large pot

→ Soil

→ Trowel

→ Medium-size tropical plant (palms work nicely)

→ Small annuals

Even city folks who don't have a yard can still garden. Clay pots or other containers allow you to dig in and garden even in a very small space. The tropical houseplant in the center of this project can be used again the following year. If you live in an area where temperatures fall below 50°F (10°C), bring the plant in the house.

* DIG IN! *

1. Fill the container a little more than halfway with soil. (Fig. 1)

2. Plant the tropical plant in the middle of the container. Before planting the annuals, place them on top of the soil to determine their spacing arrangement. Move them around until you like how they look. (Fig. 2)

3. Place the plants where you think they should go and plant them in the soil. Water them at their roots. (Fig. 3)

Fig. 1: Add the soil to the container.

Fig. 2: Arrange the spacing of the plants before planting.

Fig. 3: Plant and water your plants.

✳ DIG DEEPER! ✳
CONTAINER PLANTING

→ When planting in containers, you don't have the buffering protection of the earth like you do when planting in the ground. The plants you use in containers are subject to more temperature extremes of hot and cold, wet and dry. Because of this, think of your containers as temporary, one-year creations that you get to reinvent every spring. Depending on where you live, you can certainly plant perennials or shrubs in containers, but just know that they may not live past the first year.

* MATERIALS *

→ Paper and crayons or colored pencils

→ Shallow table top container (we used one that is 8" [20 cm] deep and 19" [48 cm] wide)

→ Soil

→ Annuals in 6 colors

A color wheel is a way to show relationships between colors.

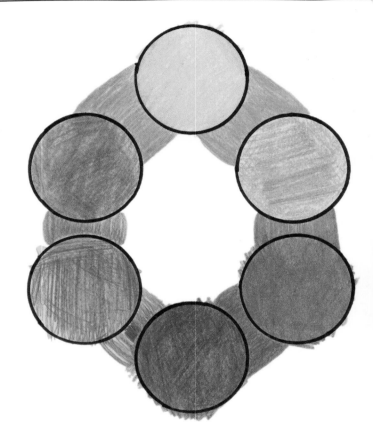

 * DIG IN! *

1. Draw six circles in a circle and color them in order: red, orange, yellow, green, blue, purple. Research plants with flowers of each of those colors and write their names in the appropriate circles. Then go shopping! (Fig. 1)

2. Fill the table top container with good potting soil. Remove the plants from their containers and loosen the roots. (Fig. 2)

Fig. 1: Make your own color wheel.

Fig. 2: Fill the container with soil.

Fig. 3: Plant and water the flowers.

3. Place the annuals in the order of the color wheel and plant them. Give them a good drink of water and place the container in the center of the table to enjoy. (Fig. 3)

☀ DIG DEEPER! ☀
LEARNING ABOUT COLORS THROUGH GARDENING

→ The primary colors of red, yellow, and blue are found at equal distances from each other around the color wheel. When two primary colors are combined, they form the secondary colors of purple, orange, and green.

→ When designing a garden, it is common to choose colors that are directly across from each other on the color wheel. Purple and yellow, blue and orange, or red and green are contrasting complementary color combinations and can add a bit of excitement in a garden when planted together.

→ Colors next to each other on the color wheel are called harmonious combinations and can be soothing or calming when planted together. Blue and green, or red and orange look very nice together.

→ Colors are also considered either "warm" or "cool." Can you guess which is which?

LAB №18 | MINI PIZZA GARDEN

Who doesn't love pizza? And when you combine the best food ever with gardening, it can't be beat. Here, we design and plant a garden dedicated to pizza so you can have fresh ingredients for a delightful meal.

* DIG IN! *

1. Poke the big stick into the ground in the center of the area where the pizza garden will be. Tie the string to the big stick near the ground. Attach the little stick to the free end of the string. Drag the little stick through the soil in a circle. This is the outside edge of your pizza garden. (Fig. 1)

2. Divide the circle into four even sections for planting. (Fig. 2)

Fig. 1: Measure the perimeter circle of your garden.

Fig. 2: Divide the circle into four "slices."

Fig. 3: Plant at the right time of year.

3. At the center of the slices, plant your onion sets in early spring. In late spring/early summer, plant the tomato, pepper, basil, and oregano in each slice. Stake your tomato plants to prevent them from falling over. Make your own, or get a tomato cage from the store. (Fig. 3)

4. Add mulch to edge the garden to represent the crust. Keep the garden watered, and harvest your bounty later in the summer. (See photo on page 56.)

⁎ DIG DEEPER! ⁎

MMM . . . PIZZA!

→ Pizza originated in Italy hundreds of years ago. It was mainly the food of the working class, who would throw the ingredients onto a piece of flatbread, bake it, eat it quickly with their hands, and go back to work. When Italian immigrants traveled to the United States, they brought this creation with them. Nonimmigrants fell in love with the taste and smell, and the love affair with pizza officially began.

→ Pizza can be healthy! We are able to absorb more of the lycopene present in tomatoes when they are cooked. Lycopene helps you have super eyesight!

LAB № 19 | SALSA GARDEN

* MATERIALS *

→ 1 kitchen sponge

→ Scissors

→ 3 medium to large pots

→ Paint: red, green, white, yellow

→ Potting soil

→ Plants: tomato, bell pepper, jalapeño (or hotter pepper), cilantro

Making fresh salsa is easy and so yummy. Even better is growing the ingredients yourself. Follow the instructions below for decorating your pots. Plant the tomato, the bell pepper, and the hot pepper in individual pots. Tuck the cilantro in next to the hot pepper plant. Water the plants well.

 * DIG IN! *

1. Cut the kitchen sponge into three 1" (2.5 cm) square pieces, and one triangle. Use the squares to paint squares of red, green, and white all over the pots. These represent the tomato, pepper, and onion chunks that will be in your salsa. (Fig. 1)

2. Paint yellow triangles on the pots using the triangle piece of sponge. These represent the tortilla chips! (Fig. 2)

3. Fill the containers with good potting mix and make sure they're positioned in full sun. (Fig. 3)

Fig. 1: Paint red, white, and green squares n the pots.

Fig. 2: Paint yellow triangles.

Fig. 3: Fill the containers with soil.

* DIG DEEPER! *
MAKE SALSA

INGREDIENTS:

Tomato
Garlic
Bell pepper
Hot pepper
Onion

Salt
Black pepper
Lime juice
Olive oil
Cilantro

DIRECTIONS:

Chop up 2 tomatoes, 1 clove of garlic, ½ bell pepper, 1 hot pepper, ½ onion, and mix together. Add salt and pepper to taste. Add a splash of lime juice and olive oil. Chop up a big bunch of cilantro and mix everything together. Refrigerate and give the flavors at least an hour to blend. Taste the salsa on a chip and add more of any of the ingredients until it tastes to your liking.

→ Did you know there is a "heat index" for peppers? Called the Scoville Scale, after Wilbur Scoville who created it in 1912, it is a heat ranking of peppers from mildest to hottest. A sweet bell pepper ranks at the bottom at 0, whereas the hottest pepper, the Trinidad Moruga Scorpion, measures 1,200,000 to 2,000,000 Scoville units. Jalapeños range from 3,500 to 8,000 Scoville units, and cayenne peppers from 30,000 to 50,000 Scoville units.

→ The heat from peppers comes from the amount of capsaicin (cap-SAY-sin) in them. Capsaicin is a natural chemical that causes a burning feeling when it comes in contact with your skin, mouth, or eyes.

* MATERIALS *

→ 50 to 60 bricks, approximately

→ Soil, gravel, sand

→ Herbs for planting: sage, rosemary, chamomile, fennel, oregano, thyme, basil, parsley

An herb spiral is a creative way of planting a lot of herbs in a really small space. Herbs love sunshine, so make sure this garden is built in full sun. Because you will want to use these herbs in cooking, locate it close to the house so you can grab a bunch to help with meal prep.

Fig. 1: Set down cardboard and newspaper.

* DIG IN! *

1. If building the herb spiral on top of grass, lay down cardboard and newspapers first to smother the grass. This will decompose over time. Use cardboard from old boxes. Don't use the glossy sheets from the newspaper. (Fig. 1)

2. Begin your spiral by placing bricks end to end in a slight curve on top of the area where the grass has been smothered. Make the base a circle approximately 3' (91 cm) across. (Fig. 2)

3. Continue by stacking bricks on top of each other. Add gravel and sand as you go to help keep the bricks in place. This also creates good drainage for the plants. (Fig. 3)

g. 2: Place the bricks in a spiral.

Fig. 3: Fill with gravel and sand.

Fig. 4: Fill with soil mixed with sand.

4. Once you reach the top, add the soil in between the bricks where the plants will go. Mix in some sand with the soil to increase drainage. Arrange the herbs in the locations you want to plant them (see below). Remove them from their containers, separate their roots, and plunk them in place. Add more soil as needed to cover the roots and water them. (Fig. 4) You may also want to cut away any of the cardboard or newspaper that is sticking out beyond the bricks. Do this carefully with a utility knife.

✳ DIG DEEPER! ✳
THE RIGHT MICROCLIMATE FOR YOUR HERBS

→ Many herbs need eight to ten hours of sun every day, but some do fine with less. Plant herbs such as the following on the north side of the herb spiral so they will get some shade from the plants in front of them: parsley, thyme, dill, fennel, chives.

→ Microclimates are small patches of a garden that are cooler or warmer than most of the surrounding area. These can be created by blocking wind, or planting next to a south facing structure that absorbs more heat through the day, and so on. Herb spirals create microclimates, too. The side facing the south will be warmer than the northern exposure. And the bricks will absorb heat throughout the day and release that heat to the plants throughout the night.

* MATERIALS *

→ 4 used tires (Tip: Poke holes in the sides for drainage and to prevent mosquitos from breeding.)

→ Indoor/outdoor white primer/sealer (Glidden Gripper works great)

→ Colorful exterior paint

→ Paint brush

→ Lots of soil

→ Seed potatoes

Used tires can be an eyesore, a health hazard, a mosquito factory, and all of the above. Why not keep some out of the disposal facility while building a perfect potato farm? By planting a few pieces of one potato, you'll have dozens of spuds to harvest in the fall!

* DIG IN! *

1. Clean the dirt from the tires, and follow the primer directions for painting and drying. Once the primer is dry, get creative with painting each tire. Allow the tires to dry overnight. (Fig. 1)

2. Place the first tire in your chosen location and fill it with soil, almost to its top. Fill the inside of the tire with soil, too. (Fig. 2)

Fig. 1: Paint the tires.

Fig. 2: Fill each tire with soil.

Fig. 3: Add tires and soil throughout the season.

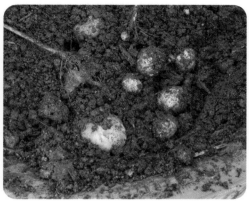

Fig. 4: Dig through soil to harvest potatoes.

3. Make sure each potato chunk has one to two eyes. These eyes will help the potatoes reproduce during the the season. Place each with the eyes facing upward in the soil, cover them with 2" to 3" (5 to 7.5 cm) of more soil, and water well. (See opening photo on page 62.)

4. Once your potatoes have reached 6" to 8" (15 to 20 cm) tall, place a second tire on top of the first, and add soil so only 2" to 4" (5 to 10 cm) of the potato plant is showing. Continue doing this throughout the season. (Fig. 3)

5. In the fall, and two weeks after the foliage has died back, remove the tires, dig through the soil, and harvest your potatoes! (Fig. 4)

* DIG DEEPER! *

THE DIRT ABOUT POTATOES

→ Potatoes originated in South America and have more potassium than bananas.

→ The part of the potato plant we eat is called a tuber, which is an enlarged, underground stem.

→ The potato is closely related to the tomato. Is that why they rhyme?

→ The largest potato on record weighed more than 7 lbs (3175 g). That's a super spud.

UNIT № 04

* GREEN GARDENING *

You would think that ALL gardening would be considered "green" or good for the planet, right? Most of it certainly is. Anytime you plant a tree, or compost something instead of throwing it out, it is definitely good for the environment. When you learn about and allow wildlife to live in your garden, it helps increase biodiversity, and collecting and using rainwater helps conserve natural resources.

Some people are convinced that to have a beautiful, thriving garden, you must use plenty of man-made fertilizers, potentially dangerous chemicals, and lots of pesticides. This simply isn't true. You can have a gorgeous and successful garden without using any chemicals and absolutely no pesticides. In addition to being much healthier for you and the environment, not using hazardous materials in your yard is also a far cheaper option.

POLLINATOR PALACE

* MATERIALS *

→ Building bricks (the ones with holes)

→ 3 pieces of pegboard, approximately 1' (30 cm) square

→ Many sticks, branches, and twigs, about 1' (30 cm) long

→ 1' (30 cm) pieces of bamboo or other hollow wood

The word *pollinator* refers to any creature that transfers pollen from the flower of one plant to another. Pollinators may be insects, birds, spiders, bats, even people. For this Lab, we are going to focus just on the pollinators with six or more legs. The ideal location for this structure is a spot that gets some sun and some shade, is away from a lot of activity, and is near some plants.

* DIG IN! *

1. In the selected location, lay two bricks down on their sides and lay one piece of pegboard on top of them. Continue with the rest of the bricks and pegboard, ending with a piece of pegboard on top for the roof. (Fig. 1)

Fig. 1: Stack the pegboard and bricks.

Fig. 2: Make sure all the materials fit together tightly.

Fig. 3: Create the roof.

2. Place larger branches in-between the bricks and then add small sticks, twigs, branches, and bamboo into the spaces between the larger branches. Fit everything tightly together so nothing moves around. (Fig. 2)

3. Finish the roof of the palace to prevent too much water from running through: Install more branches on top or get as creative as you want by adding drain tile, roofing shingles, bricks, or more branches. Sit back and wait for your pollinators to take up residence! (Fig. 3)

✷ DIG DEEPER! ✷
HELPFUL POLLINATORS

→ Insects and other pollinators are responsible for pollinating the 100 or so food crops around the world. If it wasn't for them, we wouldn't eat.

→ Domestic honeybee numbers have declined massively in the United States since 2006. Scientists aren't sure why.

→ Providing shelter for bugs can help your garden's health. Obviously, don't use chemicals near your Pollinator Palace— they aren't good for the bugs and they certainly aren't good for you!

WEE WORM BIN

* MATERIALS *

→ Plastic "shoebox" type tub, 7" to 8" (18 to 20 cm) tall, with a lid

→ Scratch awl

→ Newspapers

→ Soil

→ Red wigglers

→ Kitchen scraps— vegetable peels, etc.

Worms in your kitchen—yeah!

Although that might sound a bit odd, having a worm bin in your kitchen is a convenient way to keep food scraps out of the landfill while creating "black gold" for your garden: compost! Done correctly, there should be no smell and no fruit flies. The worms you need for this can be obtained from a mail order catalog or a local bait shop. Search on the Internet for "red wigglers" to see where to get them. And then make sure you'll be home when they are delivered!

Fig. 1: Create ventilation holes.

||||||||||||||||||||||||||||| * DIG IN! * |||||||||||||||||||||||||||||

1. Use the scratch awl to poke a line of holes near the top of the container. These are ventilation holes. (Fig. 1)

2. Rip narrow strips of newspaper (don't use the glossy sheets), dip the strips into water, and wring them out. They should be as wet as a damp sponge. This moisture level needs to be maintained, so you may periodically have to spray water into the bin. Ensure there is never standing water at the bottom. (Fig. 2)

3. Fluff up the damp newspaper and place it in the container. This should fill the tub about ¾ full. (Fig. 3)

Fig. 2: Rip and dampen newspaper.

Fig. 3: Add the dampened newspaper to the bin.

Fig. 4: Add soil to the bin.

4. Add two handfuls of moist soil to the tub. This helps the worms digest their food and gives them more places to hide. Add the worms and close the lid. Your worms need some time to adjust to their new "digs" (see what we did there?!), so ignore them for a day or two. Then you can start feeding them. Take pictures daily to document the food scraps disappearing. (Fig. 4)

5. After several weeks, your worms will have created castings (worm poop!) that you can use in your garden. (See opening photo on page 68.)

✳ DIG DEEPER! ✳
CARING FOR YOUR WORMS

▶ Things to feed your worms: vegetable and fruit scraps (making sure there is no salad dressing, sauces, or seasonings on them), coffee grounds, wet bread, or cooked pasta.

▶ Things not to feed your worms: meat, sugar, salt, citrus, dairy, and processed foods. The smaller the scraps are that you put into the bin, the faster they will begin to decompose, and the sooner your worms will start to eat them.

→ Once you become a pro worm-keeper, your worms will reproduce, increasing your population. Because these worms are adapted to living in a very rich, fluffy, organic place, they may not do well if released into your outdoor garden. The best thing to do with an overabundance of worms is to either start an additional worm bin or give some to a friend so that he or she can start a worm bin. What a great gift, right?

* MATERIALS *

→ 10" (25 cm) clay pot

→ Paints

→ Paint brushes

→ Clear polyurethane sealer

→ Trowel

Toads (and their close relatives, frogs) are very important for the ecosystem. Both animals' main diet consists of insects, many of which are pests to food crops, such as aphids or slugs. Wouldn't it be great to attract them to your yard to keep an eye on your garden?

Fig. 1: Decorate the pot, let dry, add sealer, and let dry.

Fig. 2: Dig a small area for the pot.

1. Paint some fun designs on the clay pot and let it dry. Apply the sealer and let dry overnight. (Fig. 1)

2. Find a shady, out-of-the-way location in your garden for your toad abode. Using the trowel, dig a slight depression in the soil so that when you lay the pot on its side, it won't roll around. (Fig. 2)

3. Lay the pot on its side in the depression you dug. Fill the area around the pot with soil so that the pot will stay in place. (See photo on page 70.)

||||||||||||||||||||||||||||||||||||||||||| * **DIG DEEPER!** * |||||||||||||||||||||||||||||||||||||||||||||

HEALTHY TOADS, HEALTHY ENVIRONMENT

→ Both frogs and toads are amphibians, and are key indicators of a healthy environment. Why? Because they breathe and absorb water through their skin! If the environment is polluted, they ingest those pollutants, which can kill them or prevent them from reproducing.

→ If you aren't seeing frogs or toads in your neighborhood when there should be some around, there could be something wrong. Lawn chemicals, pollution, or acid rain could be some of the reasons.

* MATERIALS *

→ 55 gallon (208 L) barrel (make sure it is "food-grade" and cleaned thoroughly)

→ ¹⁵/₁₆" (24 mm) drill bit and drill

→ ¾" (2 cm) pipe tap (These are about $25 and can be found at hardware stores. See if you can borrow one from someone instead of buying one.)

→ ¾" (2 cm) male spigot (boiler drain)

→ ¾" (2 cm) thread (male) to ½" (1.3 cm) hose connection hose barb

→ Teflon tape

→ Crescent wrench

→ Diverter kit (see Resources on page 133)

Rain barrels are a great way to harvest FREE water for use in your garden. The average gardener can save more than 1,000 gallons (3785 L) of water each summer by installing and using a rain barrel—it saves natural resources and lots of money, too. Imagine all of the new plants you could buy with those savings!

‖‖‖‖ * DIG IN! * ‖‖‖‖

1. With a ¹⁵/₁₆" (24 mm) drill bit, drill one hole near the bottom of the barrel for the spigot (boiler drain). Drill a second hold near the top of the barrel for the hose barb. Keep in mind which side you want the top hole on to connect to the diverter from the downspout. The top hole that you drill may be on the opposite side of the barrel as the bottom hole. (Fig. 1)

2. Thread both holes with the ¾" (2 cm) pipe tap. This creates ridges in the holes for the spigot and hose barb to be tightly inserted into the rain barrel and seal against water leaking. (Fig. 2)

3. Wrap the threaded ends of the spigot and hose barb with Teflon tape. (Fig. 3)

4. Insert the spigot and hose barb into their correct holes. Use the wrench to tighten and secure them into place. (Fig. 4)

5. Cut the downspout and attach the diverter according to the kit directions, fitting the hose into the hose barb. Water will continue flowing through the downspout, but now some will also be diverted into the barrel. Paint your rain barrel. (Fig. 5)

Fig. 1: Drill holes for the spigot and hose barb.

Fig. 2: Thread both holes with the pipe tap.

Fig. 3: Tape the ends of the spigot and hose barb.

Fig. 4: Tighten and secure the spigot and hose barb.

TIP: You'll need to elevate your rain barrel (cinder blocks work well for this) for several reasons:

• The higher the rain barrel is, the better water pressure you will get.

• Putting your rain barrel on stable ground and elevated will prevent it from sinking into the ground. A filled barrel weighs more than 400 lbs (181 kg).

• If the rain barrel is too close to the ground, you won't be able to fit a watering can under the spout.

Fig. 5: Attach the diverter to the cut downspout and insert.

⁂ DIG DEEPER! ⁂

MAINTAIN YOUR RAIN BARREL

→ If you live in a climate with winters below freezing, you'll need to disconnect your rain barrel each fall and store it for the season. This is a good time to empty it and clean it all out so it will be ready for the spring.

→ To further save water, use mulch in your garden to slow water evaporation from the soil and keep your plants nice and happy.

→ Get artistic with your rain barrel and paint a design on it! (See photo on page 72 for inspiration!)

* MATERIALS *

→ 3 wooden pallets

→ Paint (lots of different colors, exterior house paint works best)

→ Paint brush that will get trashed

→ 4 corner braces, screws, and screwdriver and/or drill

→ Gloves (optional)

Decide on the location for your compost bin. It should receive some sunlight and not be right next to the house. Also consider that how you paint your compost bin may depend on how often you see it. You may not want crazy colors staring back at you when you look outside!

TIP: Ask your local grocer or store manager for wooden pallets; most of the time they are glad to see them go to a good home. Pallets can be very rough and cause splinters, so you may want to wear gloves when handling them.

Fig. 1: Paint one side of each pallet.

* DIG IN! *

1. Paint one side of each of the pallets and let dry. You can paint it all one color or get creative. Only paint the outside of the compost bin. (Fig. 1)

2. Your pallets will be the sides of your bin (it will be open at the bottom). Assemble them at right angles and insert the screws and braces into the corners. (Fig. 2)

Fig. 2: Assemble the sides and attach them with braces.

Fig. 3: Add green plant material.

Fig. 4: Turn your compost regularly.

3. Start filling the bin. First add about 6" (15 cm) of small sticks and branches at the bottom to help with drainage.

4. On top of this, add 6" (15 cm) of fresh plant material, such as dried leaves or sticks. Then add 3" (8 cm) of fresh plant material, such as green leaves, grass clippings, weeds (without seeds), or kitchen scraps. (Fig. 3)

5. Use a pitchfork or shovel to mix the pile once a week for speedier results and to prevent stinky conditions. After several weeks, you'll be able to collect fantastic, homemade compost from the bottom of the pile to use in your garden. (Fig. 4)

✱ DIG DEEPER! ✱
TAKING THE STINK OUT OF COMPOSTING

→ Some people don't compost because they think it is "stinky." Actually, if you compost correctly, there is no smell. There should be a combination of two parts brown things (e.g., dried leaves) to one part green things (e.g., kitchen compost). Your compost pile should also stay moist and will heat up from all of the microbes busy eating away in the pile. Too many grass clippings decreases the amount of air spaces in the pile and can create anaerobic conditions, causing a stinky pile.

MAKE A COLD FRAME

* MATERIALS *

→ Pieces of redwood or cedar: For this window, we obtained one piece of cedar 1" x 12" x 8' (2.5 x 30 x 244 cm) for the back and two sides, and one piece of cedar 1" x 8" x 2' (2.5 x 20 x 61 cm) for the front.

→ Straight edge

→ Pencil

→ Circular saw

→ 8 corner wood braces

→ 32 wood screws

→ Screwdriver

→ 2 hinges and screws

→ 1 old glass window (this one measured 21" x 27" (53 x 68.5 cm)

→ 10" to 12" (25 to 30 cm) stick

A cold frame is an enclosure used to protect plants from cold weather. It has a transparent top to allow sunlight in to warm the plants inside, acting like a small greenhouse. Cold frames aren't used during warm summer months (it would be too hot for plant growth), just during cooler times of year. They help gardeners get a jump on the upcoming growing season and to grow things later into the fall. Select a location for your cold frame—a south-facing side of a building is best.

Fig. 5: Prop open the cold frame on warm days

Note: When using an old window, make sure it doesn't contain lead paint or pressure-treated wood. When purchasing wood, measure around all sides of the window; that is the total length of wood you will need. For example, if the window is 3' (91 cm) long and 2' (61 cm) wide, you would need 10' (305 cm) of wood (3 + 3 + 2 + 2 = 10).

* DIG IN! *

Fig. 1: Measure each side piece and draw a cutting guide.

1. Start making the box frame. Because the window will be tilted down in front slightly, the two side pieces of wood will be cut at an angle. The front of the side pieces will be the height of the front board the back of the side pieces will angle up to the height of the back board. Measure and mark each side piece accordingly. Use a straight edge to draw a straight line from this mark to the top of the other end, creating an angled piece of wood. (Fig. 1)

2. With adult assistance, use a circular saw to cut each of the four pieces of wood along the line you drew. (Fig. 2)

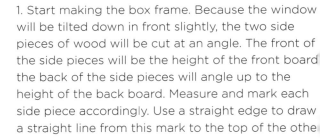

Fig. 2: Cut the four pieces of wood.

Fig. 3: Attach the wood pieces.

Fig. 4: Attach the hinges to the frame and the window.

3. Position each piece of wood at a right angle to the next to create an angled box with the tallest piece of wood as the back of the cold frame. Fasten a corner wood brace 1" (2.5 cm) from the top and 1" (2.5 cm) from the bottom inside each corner. Use the wood screws and a screw driver to attach the pieces to each other. (Fig. 3)

4. Attach the hinges to the outside, top back of the frame, then attach the window to the hinges. (Fig. 4) Place plants inside the cold frame. On warmer or sunnier days, use a stick to prop the window up a bit so it doesn't get too hot inside and bake your plants. (See photo on page 76.)

✳ DIG DEEPER! ✳
EXTEND THE SEASON

→ Making a cold frame can be as simple or as complicated as you wish to make it. We are doing a very simple version of one here, and once you get the idea, you can experiment with building something different.

→ Unless you live in an area where you can grow year-round, you might want to investigate how to grow things earlier in the season as well as later in the season. This is called "season extension," and your cold frame can help you do it.

→ Because of the window acting as a lid, rain won't be able to enter the cold frame. This means you are responsible for watering any plants inside. During very cool months, many plants are dormant and don't need much, if any, water.

* MATERIALS *

→ Wire hanger

→ Duct tape

→ ¾" (2 cm) wooden dowel

→ 1 yard (91.5 cm) tulle fabric

→ Needle and thread

→ Small, clean glass jar with lid (poke small holes in the lid)

→ Insect identification book or insect ID app on a mobile device

Bugs are incredibly important to a successful garden, and most bugs you find in a garden are beneficial, or good, bugs. Take some time to introduce yourself to your insect residents and learn a little bit about them.

* DIG IN! *

1. "Round out" the triangle part of the wire clothes hanger, straighten out the hook part, and duct tape like crazy the now straight part to the wooden dowel. (Fig. 1)

2. Fold the tulle in half and cut a triangle as shown. Stitch the long open sides together. (Fig. 2)

3. Fold the circular opening of the net over the round part of the wire hanger, overlapping by 1" (2.5 cm). Stitch all the way around to hold it in place. You now have an insect net! (Fig. 3)

Fig. 1: Tightly tape the straight part of the hanger to the dowel rod.

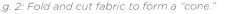

Fig. 2: Fold and cut fabric to form a "cone."

Fig. 3: Loop fabric over the wire hanger and sew it in place.

Fig. 4: Identify the bug in the jar and release it when done.

4. In the garden, use a gentle sweeping motion of the net to capture an insect you want to closely study, as shown in the opening photo on page 78. Gently deposit the insect you catch into the glass jar and close the lid. Use your ID guides to find out what kind of insect you captured. It is probably a "good guy," so open the lid and put him back where you captured him and say thank you! (Fig. 4)

✳ DIG DEEPER! ✳
CREATE A BUG-FRIENDLY GARDEN

→ Encourage helpful insects to visit your garden by growing plants they need to live. For example, to attract lacewings to your yard, plant fennel, yarrow, or dill. Lady beetles (lady bugs) also love a good yarrow or dill, in addition to Queen Anne's lace and coriander. An additional bonus is that these plants that attract beneficial insects are lovely as well!

* MATERIALS *

→ Old wooden picture frame about 8" x 10" (20 x 25.4 cm)

→ Drill and tiny drill bit

→ 4 small screw eyes

→ Piece of screening slightly bigger than your picture frame

→ Staple gun and staples

→ 5 small "S" hooks

→ 10' (304 cm) of rope chain

Bird watching is the number one activity in many parts of the world, and it's easy to see why. Birds come in all colors and sizes, and their behaviors are interesting and sometimes comical to watch! By making a feeder for the birds and hanging it near a window, you can attract them close for convenient, indoor viewing.

* DIG IN! *

1. Drill guide holes in each corner on the back of the picture frame. (Fig. 1)

2. Using the holes you drilled, set the screw eyes into place. (Fig. 2)

3. Center the screening over the picture frame. Use the staple gun to fix it in place. Make sure you staple the screening near the corners of the frame. (Fig. 3)

Fig. 1: Drill the guide holes.

Fig. 2: Insert the screw eyes.

Fig. 3: Center and staple the screening into the frame.

Fig. 4: Attach the rope chain to the feeder.

4. Loop an "S" hook through each screw eye. Then loop a 2' (61 cm) section of rope chain through each "S" hook, gathering each piece together and looping them through the fifth "S" hook. Hang the feeder by attaching the rest of the rope to the "S" hook. Fill the feeder with seed and hang outside to enjoy. Your feathered friends will thank you. (Fig. 4)

✳ DIG DEEPER! ✳
HELP NATIVE BIRDS

→ Research the native birds of your area; a good place to start is your state's department of natural resources website. Learn what your native birds need for survival and help provide that for them. Planting perennials, shrubs, and trees that provide food and shelter for them year-round is ideal. Provide clean water for them to drink and bathe in by making your own birdbath (Lab 38).

→ Native birds are important to the ecosystem as pollinators, insect and rodent control, distributing seeds, and many other reasons. The biggest threat to native birds is the domestic cat. Cats kill millions of songbirds every year. The best way to prevent this is to keep cats indoors, which keeps cats safe, too.

Most of us are not blessed with weather that allows us to garden outside year-round. But you can still get your plant fix by gardening indoors. Use a container that has a wide opening so you don't have to cut the top to get all of your materials inside. Make sure you've cleaned the container well with soap and water before starting.

* MATERIALS *

→ Sheet of paper

→ Clear, lidded plastic or glass bottle with large top opening

→ 2 cups (490 g) gravel

→ 1 to 3 tablespoons (30 to 90 g) charcoal

→ 2 cups (200 g) potting soil

→ Chopstick or other long stick

→ Cuttings from plants to propagate: Jade (Crassula), Snake plant (Sansevieria), Burro's tail (Sedum)

→ Rooting powder

→ Spray bottle

* DIG IN! *

1. Roll the paper into a funnel shape and use it to pour the gravel into the bottom of your terrarium. Gently shake bottle to spread the gravel evenly. (Fig. 1)

Fig. 1 (left): Pour in the gravel.

Fig. 2: Pour in the charcoal and soil.

Fig. 3: Dip the cuttings.

Fig. 4: Lower each plant into the bottle.

Pour charcoal onto the gravel, using a chopstick to spread it evenly on top. Pour the soil in the same way. (Fig. 2)

Decide how you want your plants arranged. Dip the stem of each plant cutting into the rooting powder. Follow directions and precautions listed on the rooting powder container. (Fig. 3)

Lower each plant into its location. (Fig. 4)

Press plants firmly into the soil, using your chopsticks. Spray water all over the inside of the bottle and put the lid back on your terrarium. (Fig. 5)

Fig. 5: Use the chopsticks to move the plants into location.

* DIG DEEPER! *
HOW TO WATER YOUR TERRARIUM

One of the coolest things about terraria (plural of terrarium) is that if done correctly, they require almost no care. It's important to put the right amounts of gravel and soil in the container you choose. The soil will hold moisture in it and the gravel helps drain too much water away to prevent your plants from getting waterlogged.

→ Newly propagated plants (like the cuttings we used here) need a bit more water when they are first planted, so growing them in a terrarium is perfect. The day after you plant them, check the terrarium to see how much water is on the sides of the container. If all of the sides are covered in big water drops, there is too much water in your terrarium. This is easily fixed by taking the lid off the container for several hours, then replacing it.

* MATERIALS *

→ Dryer lint

→ Small sticks

→ Dried grass

→ Short pieces of yarn

→ Large metal whisk

→ 8" (20 cm) piece of twine

Home is where the heart is, but when it comes to birds, home is where the nest is. Many birds use various materials to make their nests where they lay eggs and protect their young. Birds are busy, so why not collect those items for them and keep them all together in one place?

* DIG IN! *

1. Gather the miscellaneous nesting materials by searching around the yard or in the neighborhood. When collecting dried grass, do not take it from lawns that have chemicals on them. Break or cut small sticks so they are shorter than 6" (15 cm) long. Cotton yarn should be cut into pieces smaller than 4" (10 cm). (Fig. 1)

2. Push all of the materials into the whisk. Tie the twine through the handle and hang the whisk from a tree birds like to visit (maybe near the bird feeder you made in Lab 29?). (Fig. 2)

Fig. 1: Gather the nesting materials.

Fig. 2: Insert the nesting materials.

* DIG DEEPER! *
FOR THE BIRDS

> It is believed that birds evolved from dinosaurs. Makes you want to give them a little more respect, doesn't it?

> Birds have hollow bones so they are lightweight and can fly.

> Attracting birds to your garden is a win-win: Birds are so entertaining to watch, and insect-eating birds will help remove pests from your plants.

UNIT N° 05

* GARDEN ART *

Gardens are, by their very nature, works of art. Many art concepts, such as texture, line, symmetry, color, and focal point are used when designing garden spaces. Additionally, gardens are perfect places to display works of art. Beautiful backdrops of shrubs, trees, and flowers are only enhanced when an artistic creation is placed amid them. This unit will have you getting creative with paint, water, cement, and bottle caps to make unique items for your outdoor space. The messier you get, the better.

STEPPING STONES

Making your own stepping stones is an easy way of personalizing your garden
By using containers that were going to be thrown into the recycling bin anyway, you are saving the planet while saving money.

* MATERIALS *

→ Recycled plastic carryout containers no bigger than 1' (30 cm) across

→ Vegetable oil

→ Decorative stone or gravel, or marbles, etc.

→ Tub or bucket for mixing cement

→ Bag of perlite

→ Bag of peat moss

→ Bag of Portland cement

→ Dust mask

→ Rubber gloves

→ Plastic wrap

NOTE: Always wear a dust mask when working with these materials, and always wear gloves when mixing these materials together.

 * DIG IN! *

Fig. 1: Apply oil to the container.

Fig. 2: Place decorative stones.

Fig. 3: Mix the perlite, peat moss, and cement together.

Fig. 4: Add water to the mixture and mix with your hands.

Fig. 5: Scoop and press the mixture into each container.

1. Cover the insides of the containers with vegetable oil. This will help the hardened stepping stones pop out of the containers. (Fig. 1)

2. Place decorative stones or marbles into the container. (Fig. 2)

3. Mix equal parts perlite, peat moss, and Portland cement in a tub or bucket. Break up any chunks and wear a dust mask while doing this. (Fig. 3)

4. Wear gloves and slowly add water to the mixture, stirring with your hands. Ultimately you want it to be the consistency of cottage cheese—not too dry, not too wet. (Fig. 4)

5. Carefully scoop the mixture into each container, on top of the stones or gravel. Press the mixture down to push out any air bubbles. Cover the containers with plastic wrap for three to four days to cure. After several days, unwrap a stone and try pressing your fingernail into it. If you can't make an indentation, then it is ready to carefully remove from the container. (Fig. 5)

✳ DIG DEEPER! ✳
CARING FOR YOUR STEPPING STONES

→ The mixture used in this Lab, called hypertufa, takes several weeks to completely cure, so keep the stepping stones out of direct sunlight until then. While they cure, misting them with water regularly helps strengthen and prevent them from cracking.

→ If you live where winter temperatures are below freezing, bring your stepping stones inside during the cold months to extend their life.

LAB № 33 | WIND CHIMES

* MATERIALS *

→ 42 metal bottle caps

→ Piece of scrap wood

→ Scratch awl
(or a roofing nail)

→ Hammer

→ 1/8" (3 mm) wide ribbon

→ Tapestry needle

→ Plastic lid from coffee
container

→ 7 buttons or beads

→ Metal twist tie

Wind chimes are whimsical ornaments that add pleasant sounds and movement to your garden.
Making them is fun and allows for lots of creativity in the materials you use. Here we are using some upcycling items that otherwise may have been thrown away. Before starting, arrange your materials on a flat surface and lay out newspaper.

|||||| * DIG IN! * ||||||

1. Place bottle caps upside down on the piece of scrap wood. Aim the awl or nail at the rubber seal and hammer it into the cap to punch a hole. Remove the awl and continue with each bottle cap. (Fig. 1)

2. Cut seven 36" (91 cm) pieces of ribbon. Using the tapestry needle, thread the ribbon through the hole on a bottle cap and tie a double knot just above the cap to keep it in place. (Fig. 2)

3. Continue adding five more bottle caps at different spacing along the length of the ribbon. Leave 6" (15 cm) of ribbon at the end. (Fig. 3)

4. Use the awl to punch holes into the plastic lid. Once you have seven lengths of ribbon threaded with caps, thread each ribbon through a hole in the plastic lid, knotting the ribbon once through a button or bead to hold it in place. (Fig. 4)

5. Gather all of the loose ends of ribbon together and wrap the metal twist tie around them to their ends. Wrap it around on itself to form a loop and secure the ends. (Fig. 5)

Fig. 1: Punch holes in the bottle caps.

Fig. 2: Thread and knot the ribbon.

Fig. 3: Add more caps to the ribbon.

Fig. 4: Thread the ribbon through the plastic
[li]d and knot it.

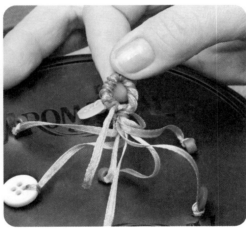

Fig. 5: Wrap the twist tie around the loose
ribbon ends.

✳ DIG DEEPER! ✳
UPCYCLING

→ Upcycling is an environmental way of reusing otherwise useless materials and turning them into something functional. Look around for other materials you could upcycle and use in your garden. What are some things you normally throw away or recycle that you could use? Keep a list of items for possible projects in your garden journal (Lab 42).

* MATERIALS *

→ Large lids from glass jars

→ Scratch awl

→ Permanent marker

→ Wire hangers

→ Needle nose pliers

Once your garden is growing and beautiful and full of gorgeous greenery, people will want to know the names of every plant in it. You will probably remember many, if not all, but sometimes we just plain forget. Make and display these upcycled plant labels so people can see what you are growing. Learn a little Latin while you're at it, too.

Fig. 1: Poke two holes in each lid.

* DIG IN! *

1. Use the scratch awl to make a hole in the inside edge of a lid. This will be the top of the plant label. Poke another hole on the opposite side (the bottom) to allow water to drain out. (Fig. 1)

2. Using the permanent marker, write the common name of a plant in the center of the inside of a lid. If you also know the Latin name of the plant, write that along the bottom of the lid. (Fig. 2)

3. Straighten the wire hanger. Use the pliers to cut it into three equal segments. (Fig. 3)

4. Loop the wire through the top of the top hole. Wrap the wire around the back of the lid so the lid hangs from it. Push the wire into the ground near the plant and you're ready for garden tours! (Fig. 4)

Fig. 2: Write the plant name on the lid.

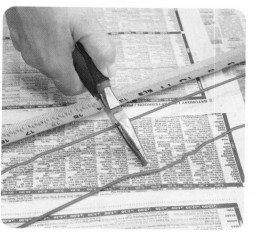
Fig. 3: Cut the hanger into three equal pieces.

Fig. 4: Insert wire into the lid.

* DIG DEEPER! *
LEARN SOME LATIN

→ Oh Latin names, how I love thee. All living things in the universe have a Latin name that consists of two words. Human beings are called *Homo sapiens*, which translates to "wise man." All Latin names are italicized and the first word is always capitalized. The first word is the *genus*, the second is the *species*.

→ Organisms are given a scientific or Latin name so that each living thing has only one correct name. If you are in Ohio talking about *Echinacea purpurea*, your friend in Belgium knows you're looking at the Eastern purple coneflower.

→ Scientific names differ from common names in that every organism has only one scientific name but may have many common names. For example, *Actaea simplex* is also commonly known as baneberry, snakeroot, purple snakeroot, autumn bugbane, black cohosh, bugbane, and autumn snakeroot!

→ Here are just a handful of Latin roots and their meanings. The next time you read a plant label at a nursery, you'll know more about the plant from its name if any of these are a part of it:

Alba – white
Acer – sharp
Crassula - thick
Barbata – bearded, hairy
Dura – hard
Echinos – hedgehog, porcupine
Eros – love, heart-shaped
Eximia – excellent

Flavus – yellow
Ferox – strongly armed with teeth (Yikes!)
Glabrus – smooth
Magna – big
Rubra – red
Vulgaris – common

* MATERIALS *

→ Empty soup can, label removed

→ Old towel

→ Scratch awl

→ Hammer

→ 18 gauge wire

Tip: If you do not want to use these as hangers, fill the bottom of each can with 1" (2.5cm) of sand to add weight and prevent them from blowing over when there is a candle inside.

Lanterns and luminaries are ancient ways of lighting spaces. The early Greeks and Romans used them to see at night and provide some security. A luminary is defined as "a body that gives off light." It can also be defined as "an important person of prominence and achievement." So when you complete this Lab, can you be called a "Luminary Luminary"?

* DIG IN! *

1. Fill the can with water and place in the freezer overnight. This step makes it easier to poke holes into the sides of the can without the can collapsing into itself. Don't leave it in there much longer as the can may split open. (Fig. 1)

2. Remove the can from the freezer. Lay it on its side on the folded up towel. The towel will help hold the can in place while you work. (Fig. 2)

3. Use the scratch awl and hammer to poke two holes at the top of each can directly across from each other. These will be used for hanging the luminaries. (Fig. 3)

4. Starting 1" (2.5 cm) from the bottom of the can, carefully use the scratch awl and hammer to pound holes randomly all over the can. (Fig. 4)

5. Loop the wire through the two holes at the top for hanging. (Fig. 5)

Fig. 1: Fill the can with water and freeze.

Fig. 2: Lay the can on its side on the towel.

Fig. 3: Make openings at the top of the can for hanging.

Fig. 4: Hold the awl above the can and hit the base of it with the hammer to make holes.

Fig. 5: Loop the wire through the top holes and secure it.

* DIG DEEPER! *
LUMINARY TIPS

→ Use tealights in your luminaries, and never leave them unattended when lit. Use only with adult supervision or battery run lights.

→ Did you know some plants are flammable? Pines, junipers, and firs are very flammable, and open flame should not be used near them.

→ Draw a design on the cans with a grease pencil, then poke holes in the can following the design. When done, wipe the excess grease pencil markings off.

MAKE A SWEET PEA TEEPEE

* MATERIALS *

→ 4' (122 cm) sections of bamboo or similar wooden sticks

→ Rubber band

→ Colorful twine

→ Dandelion weeder or similar metal pokey thing

→ Sweet pea seeds

Sure, you can buy a cheap boring trellis for your climbing plants to explore. But even better is making your own fun structure for these cute flowers. If you were a sweet pea, wouldn't you want to climb up this?

 * DIG IN! *

1. Gather the bamboo sticks and keep them together by wrapping the rubber band around them three to four times until tight, about 3" (7.5 cm) from the ends of the sticks. Wrap the twine around the rubber band, covering it completely. (Fig. 1)

2. Spread the other ends of the bamboo out in a circle in the location you'll be planting the seeds. Use the dandelion weeder to poke holes in the ground for the sticks. Push the sticks firmly into the soil—you don't want it to come crashing down while your flowers are growing! (Fig. 2)

3. Plant two to three seeds at the base of each pole, following package directions, and water them in well. (Fig. 3)

Fig. 1: Wrap the rubber band around the bamboo. Then wrap the twine.

Fig. 2: Arrange the ends of the sticks into a circle.

Fig. 3: Plant and water your seeds.

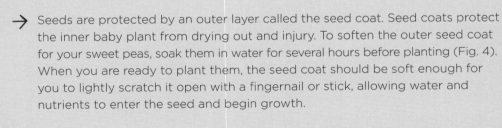

* DIG DEEPER! *
SEED COATS OF ARMOR

→ Seeds are protected by an outer layer called the seed coat. Seed coats protect the inner baby plant from drying out and injury. To soften the outer seed coat for your sweet peas, soak them in water for several hours before planting (Fig. 4). When you are ready to plant them, the seed coat should be soft enough for you to lightly scratch it open with a fingernail or stick, allowing water and nutrients to enter the seed and begin growth.

→ Some seed coats are so strong they have to pass through the stomach acids of animals or live through a forest fire for the seed to grow!

Fig. 4: Soak sweet pea seeds before planting.

→ Plastic containers of various shapes and sizes, some large, some smaller

→ Vegetable oil

→ Bag of perlite

→ Bag of Portland cement

→ Bag of peat moss

→ Bucket or other large container

→ Dust mask

→ Rubber gloves

→ Plastic straw

→ Scissors

→ Plastic wrap

NOTE: Always wear a dust mask when working with these materials and gloves when mixing them together.

For this Lab, use containers that nest inside one another so there is less than an inch (2.5 cm) in between them. Let's call the bigger container in each pair the "nester" and the smaller one the "nestee."

||||||| * DIG IN! * |||||||

1. For each pair of containers, oil the inside of each nester and the outside of each nestee. This will help you remove the hardened hypertufa from the container. (Fig. 1)

2. Add equal parts perlite, cement, and peat moss to the bucket. Wear a dust mask and gloves and mix together using your hands. Break up any big clumps and remove any sticks. (Fig. 2)

3. Slowly add water to the mixture and carefully mix it with your hands (still wearing a mask and gloves!). Your end product should be smooth and not very wet. (Fig. 3)

4. Scoop some hypertufa mixture into the bottom of one of the nesters, so that it is abo 1" (2.5 cm) deep. Cut a length from the plastic straw the same height and press it into the center of the mixture. This will be the drainage hole once you remove the straw afte drying. (Fig. 4)

5. Insert the smaller container into the bigger, slightly pressing into the hypertufa mixtur at the bottom. Scoop more hypertufa in between the two containers, filling to the top o the inner container. Smooth the top surface. (Fig. 5)

6. Cover each set of containers with plastic wrap. Remove the nestees the next day. Let them dry or "cure" for several more days. The plastic wrap helps hold in moisture so that the hypertufa dries slowly and strong. If you can scrape into the mixture with your fingernail, let it sit longer. (Fig. 6)

Fig. 1: Oil the containers.

Fig. 2: Mix the perlite, cement, and peat moss with your hands.

Fig. 3: Add water and mix.

Fig. 4: Add hypertufa mixture to the container. Press a straw into the center.

Fig. 5: Place the nestee into the nester and add hypertufa mixture.

Fig. 6: Cover the containers for several days.

* DIG DEEPER! *
LOSE THE LIME!

→ When your hypertufa containers are completely cured (which, depending on their size, could take several weeks to several months), submerge them in water for several days to remove some of the lime in them from the cement. Large quantities of lime aren't good for plants.

* MATERIALS *

→ Shallow bowl or dish

→ Waterproof silicone

→ Candlestick

Let your creative juices roll for this activity! Visit garage sales or thrift stores to buy crazy bowls and candlesticks very cheaply. It's fun to completely mismatch styles and be as imaginative as you want. These can also make great gifts!

* DIG IN! *

1. Cover your work surface and lay out your materials. Lay your bowl upside down on the table. (Fig. 1)

2. Squeeze a line of silicone completely around the top of the candlestick. Make sure it is a continuous bead of silicone so you have a complete, watertight seal when it dries. (Fig. 2)

Fig. 1: Gather your materials.

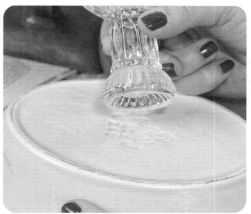

Fig. 2: Line the top of the candlestick with the silicone.

Fig. 3: Press the candlestick to the bowl and let it dry.

Fig. 4: Enjoy your birdbath!

3. Press the candlestick onto the center of the bottom of the bowl. Let this dry upside down overnight. (Fig. 3)

4. Once completely dry, place the birdbath in your garden and fill with water for your birds to enjoy! Replace the water every other day so your birds have fresh, clean water. (Fig. 4)

✳ DIG DEEPER! ✳
BIRD FACTS

→ Did you know birds can't sweat? Flopping around in your birdbath will help keep them cool during the hot days of summer. Also, birds need to keep their feathers clean and in perfect condition so they can fly.

→ Birds aren't all that crazy about new things, so it may take them a couple of weeks to start enjoying their birdbath. Place it near a bird feeder (Lab 29) or a shrub they congregate in. This may help them get accustomed to their new work of art sooner.

→ Depending on what your birdbath is made of, it probably cannot withstand winter cold without cracking. Remember to bring it inside when temperatures are expected to be below 32°F (0°C).

PLAYING WITH POTS

* MATERIALS *

→ Newspapers for the work surface

→ Acrylic paints in several different colors

→ Paper plate

→ Natural paint sponges

→ Clay pots (We used 2" to 4" [5 to 10 cm] pots, but you can pick any size you want.)

→ Fun paper

→ Line of poetry or a saying you like

→ Water-based sealer (Mod Podge works well)

→ Foam brushes

→ Polyurethane

I love the color and look of plain, old clay pots. But sometimes you just want a little bit more zip. This Lab unleashes your creativity to make lovely works of art for your garden or for gifts. Before starting, wipe any dust or dirt off of the pot using a damp paper towel and allow it to dry. Cover your work surface with newspaper.

* DIG IN! *

1. Squirt two to four different colors of paint onto the paper plate. (Fig. 1)

2. Dip the sponge into the paint, then dab it onto the pot in lovely randomness. Leave lots of empty space. Repeat with the other colors, allowing drying time between coats. (Fig. 2)

3. Type up and print the saying you want on the pot. Rip the paper into a thin strip that will fit around the rim of the pot. Brush the water-based sealer onto the rim, apply the paper, then brush more sealer over the paper to seal it. Allow this to dry. (Fig. 3)

4. Apply the polyurethane sealer to the entire pot, inside and out, to prevent the paint from chipping or peeling. Allow to dry. (Fig. 4)

Fig. 1: Dispense paint onto the plate.

Fig. 2: Sponge paint the pot.

Fig. 3: Print a saying on a thin strip of paper and affix it to the pot rim.

Fig. 4: Seal the pot with polyurethane.

✳ DIG DEEPER! ✳
MAKE A CLEVER WEDDING FAVOR

→ I know someone who made these pots for wedding favors. She had a lovely Native American proverb, along with the couple's wedding date, on the piece of paper on the rim. Because it was a fall wedding, she bought tons of crocus bulbs (her favorite), wrapped them in burlap, tied them with twine, and put each bundle into a pot. Oh, yeah! That was me.

* MATERIALS *

→ Photos of bugs

→ Smooth rocks in different shapes and sizes

→ Pencil

→ Acrylic paint in all sorts of colors

→ Small paintbrushes

→ Polyurethane

→ Foam brush

Bugs are important to have in the garden: they pollinate, protect biodiversity, eat bad things, and are themselves food for other things. In this Lab, we pay homage to these delightful little creatures by making rock images of them to adorn your garden. You can be as realistic or fanciful with your creations as you wish. Find photos of bugs online or get some bug identification books from the library.

 * DIG IN! *

1. Make sure the rocks are clean and dry. Select the type of bug you want to paint and outline its design on the rock with pencil. (Fig. 1)

2. Use the paint to fill in the design. Allow paint to dry overnight. (Fig. 2)

3. Cover the entire design with the polyurethane to preserve your creation. Allow to dry. Place your rock bugs in your garden for everyone to admire. (Fig. 3)

Fig. 1: Draw the bug on the rock.

Fig. 2: Paint your bug and allow to dry.

Fig. 3: Coat your rock bug with polyurethane.

DIG DEEPER!

LEARN MORE ABOUT BUGS

▶ When someone says the word *bugs*, he or she usually means any creepy crawly thing with a ton of legs. But by definition, an insect has six legs, three body parts, and a pair of antennae.

▶ No one knows the exact number of different kinds of insects there are in the world. Estimates range from 1 million to 30 million.

→ The largest beetle in the world is from South America and is close to 8" (20 cm) long.

→ Dragonflies can fly 35 miles per hour!

→ Brightly colored insects may be warning others they are poisonous or dangerous if angered. Insects with muted colors are usually trying to blend in with their surroundings for protection.

* MATERIALS *

→ 5 clay pots in decreasing sizes, 12" to 6" (30 to 15 cm) approximately

→ Waterproofing repair tape

→ 3 5/8" (16 mm) rubber leg tips

→ Waterproof silicone adhesive

→ Rubber tubing

→ Fountain pump

→ Small rocks, such as river rocks

There is nothing more relaxing than the sounds of gurgling water. Why not put this clay pot fountain together and enjoy the tranquility it brings to your garden? Make sure the pots are clean and dry before you start. Build your fountain next to the electrical outlet you'll use so you don't have to move it when you're done.

* DIG IN! *

1. Place the largest pot in the chosen location and use the waterproofing tape to cover the bottom drainage hole completely. Put the three rubber leg tips in the bottom of the pot equal distance from each other. Use the silicone to adhere them to the pot and allow this to dry overnight. (Fig. 1)

2. Attach the tubing to the fountain pump and place it on the bottom of the pot, in between the leg tips. Ensure the electrical cord is hanging outside the top of the base pot. (Fig. 2)

3. Place the third biggest pot upside down on top of the leg tips, threading the rubber tubing from the fountain pump through the hole. Use the waterproofing tape to seal the hole the tubing is coming out of. (Fig. 3)

Fig. 1: Tape the drainage hole and add the
g tips.

Fig. 2: Place the fountain pump above the
drainage hole.

Fig. 3: Place pot inside largest pot, thread
tubing through drainage hole, and seal.

4. Stack the biggest remaining pot right side up, on top of the upside down
pot, and thread the tubing through the drainage holes. Seal the gaps with
waterproofing tape. Continue this way until all five pots are used and the tubing is
sticking out the top of the smallest pot. Begin adding the river rocks to the pots.
Fill the pots with water and plug the pump into an electrical outlet to ensure it is
working correctly. (Fig. 4)

NOTE: Make sure your hands and the fountain plug are completely dry before
plugging into the outlet. Be careful when you do this as the water may come
shooting straight up! Then fill the pots with the rocks, experimenting with
placement for different water effects or sounds. Placing a larger rock near where
the water comes out of the end of the tubing may be needed to slow the water
flow if it is coming out too powerfully.

Fig. 4: Stack the pots until the smallest is on
top with the fountain tubing sticking through.
Seal each hole and add the river rock.

* DIG DEEPER! *

ENJOY YOUR WATER FOUNTAIN

→ Before completely filling the fountain with the river
rock, fill it with water and plug the pump in to ensure it
is working. With all of the jostling it undergoes during
the construction of the fountain, something may come
dislodged. It's easier to remove a little bit of rock than if
you had filled it completely.

→ The sound of bubbling water can mask other, unwanted
sounds and create a lovely respite in your garden.

→ Moving water can attract birds, so place your bird feeder
(Lab 29) and birdbath (Lab 38) nearby.

UNIT №= 06

✳ ENJOYING YOUR GARDEN ✳

Why have a garden? Why go through the work, sweat, tears, and mud? What's the point, if not to enjoy your garden? Yes, the act of gardening can be very relaxing, it is great exercise, you are beautifying a little corner of the world, but you also have to take time to enjoy it. There's nothing better than strolling through or sitting amid your plant paradise after a hard day of work in it. Sharing it with friends and family is a real treat, too.

It is also interesting to know that as human beings, we are wired to calm down when we see the color green. Our nervous system slows down when we are surrounded by the shades of green in our gardens. That's one of the reasons people spend time in nature: to "quiet the soul."

There is also a tremendous amount of research indicating that our bodies heal up to 50 percent faster from disease, illness, or injury when we have a view of greenery. Researchers studied patients in hospitals—those with views to an outdoor garden recovered twice as quickly as people with no view or a view of just buildings. When my mom had colon surgery in the thick of winter, I was so nervous about her recovery, and I didn't want to take any chances, that I bought a bunch of orchids and flowering spring bulbs for the windowsill in the hospital. I loaded up her view so that the goodness of plants would help her heal. I guess it worked because she went home three days after surgery!

Studies also show that even the simple act of tending to your plants—watering, weeding, deadheading, and so forth—increases a sense of well-being in people. This holds true for tending to your indoor plants as well. I know I feel great after cleaning up and watering all of my plants—don't you?

* MATERIALS *

→ Garden magazines or plant and seed catalogs

→ Foam brush

→ Water-based sealant (Mod Podge works well)

→ 1 tab file folder

→ 15 sheets of 11" x 8½" (28 x 22 cm) graph paper

→ Scratch awl

→ Tapestry needle

→ Ribbon

Yes you could certainly buy a journal to use, but that's not the point here, is it? By making your own, you can make it exactly how you want it—from the size, the type of paper, and so on—it is your very own creation. You can decorate the cover using objects from your garden; maybe some pressed leaves after you complete Lab 47?

* DIG IN! *

1. Rip out strips from the gardening magazines and plant catalogs. Use the foam brush to cover the strips of paper with the water-based sealant and stick them on the file folder, front and back. Let this dry overnight. (Fig. 1)

2. Fold the graph paper in half as shown. Cut the tab file folder so that it is just a bit bigger than the folded graph paper. (Fig. 2)

3. Place the folded sheets of paper into the file folder. Use the awl to punch four holes through all of the sheets and the folder. (Fig. 3)

4. From the outside of the folder, use the tapestry needle to thread the ribbon through one of the holes, pushing it back out through the next one. Tie a knot. Do the same with the other two holes. (Fig. 4)

Who's got a super cool journal now? You do. And the piece cut from the file folder becomes two super cool bookmarkers. You're welcome.

Fig. 1: Decorate the journal cover.

Fig. 2: Cut the file folder slightly larger than the graph paper.

Fig. 3: Punch holes through the paper and journal cover.

Fig. 4: Thread the ribbon through the pages and cover.

✳ DIG DEEPER! ✳

DOCUMENT YOUR GARDEN HAPPENINGS

→ Your garden journal is going to be beautiful and so very creative. But its purpose is very important. Documenting what happens in your garden is important so you remember what you've done, what grew well, and especially in northern climes, what is planted underneath all of that snow! In addition to the date of each entry, include the following information in your journal:

- What you plant
- What you cut back
- What is growing well and not so well
- What bugs or other wildlife you see

- Ideas or changes you want to make
- New plants you find out about and might want to try growing

→ Including pictures in your journal is valuable, too. You can make a sketch or take a picture to remind you of what is blooming, where a bare spot might be next year, and so on.

LAB №
43

* MATERIALS *

→ Garden journal

→ Writing instrument

→ Creative juices!

Poetry can be an acquired taste, but it can also be whatever you want it to be. There are many different types of poetry, from very serious and brooding, to lively, funny, and silly. Let your garden inspire you to write a poem or three to record in your garden journal (Lab 42).

Fig. 1: Find an inspiring place in your garden.

* DIG IN! *

1. Find a space to get comfortable and inspired in your garden. This activity focuses on three types of poetry: haiku, cinquain, and acrostic. (Fig. 1)

2. Haiku is a three-lined poem, the first line consisting of five syllables, the second line having seven, and the last line with five syllables again. (Fig. 2)

3. A cinquain is a five-lined poem: Line one is one word and the title of the poem. Line two is two words describing the title. Line three is three words that express action of the title. Line four is four words that express feeling of the title. And line five is one word that restates the title a different way. (Fig. 3)

4. An acrostic is a poem uses letters of a word for the first letter of each line. Write one about your favorite plant in your garden. (Fig. 4)

5. Write a poem representing each of these and share with a friend. Research other types of poetry and poets who wrote about gardens.

I love my garden!
The plants, the flowers, the trees
Happy and peaceful.

Fig. 2: A haiku poem follows a five-seven-five syllable format.

Daisy
Sunny, happy
Swaying, growing, opening
Summer, warm, smiling, bright
Flower

Fig. 3: Create a cinquain poem of five lines.

Lovely spring flowers
In my yard
Lavender, purple, white
Amazing beauty
Colorful blessing

Fig. 4: Create an acrostic poem about your favorite plant.

DIG DEEPER!
MAGICAL LINES

Here is a lovely poem that might give you inspiration. Or it might just make you happy:

GARDEN MAGIC
This is the garden's magic,
That through the sunny hours
The gardener who tends it,
Himself outgrows his flowers.

He grows by gift of patience,
Since he who sows must know
That only in the Lord's good time
Does any seedling grow.

He learns from buds unfolding,
From each tight leaf unfurled,
That his own heart, expanding,
Is one with all the world.

He bares his head to sunshine,
His bending back a sign
Of grace, and ev'ry shower becomes
His sacramental wine.

And when at last his labors
Bring forth the very stuff
And substance of all beauty
This is reward enough.

-Marie Nettleton Carroll

A PLACE TO REST

* MATERIALS *

→ Scissors

→ 2" x 22" x 22" (5 x 56 x 56 cm) high-density foam

→ 4 yards (366 cm) outdoor fabric

→ Instant fabric and leather adhesive (Bish's Original Tear Mender works well)

→ 4 tree stumps

→ Polyurethane sealant and paint brush (optional)

Stopping and smelling the roses is good for you, so you might as well have a nice place to sit while admiring your garden. This project requires no sewing; just the skill to wrap a present.

* DIG IN! *

1. Cut the foam into four equal pieces, each measuring 11" (28 cm) square. (Fig. 1)

2. Cut a piece of fabric so it is big enough to wrap around one piece of foam like you're wrapping a present. Trim excess fabric. (Fig. 2)

3. Use the adhesive to seal the edges of the fabric and let it dry according to product directions. Place your completed cushions on the tree stumps for a handy place to sit in your garden. (Fig. 3)

4. To protect the tree stumps, seal them with polyurethane and let them dry first.

Fig. 1: Cut the foam.

Fig. 2: Cut a piece of fabric to wrap around the foam.

Fig. 3: Seal the fabric edges.

✳ DIG DEEPER! ✳
ENJOY NATURE

→ Once you find a nice spot to sit in your garden, close your eyes and breathe in and out slowly five times. As you inhale, imagine your lungs filling with good, clean air; when you exhale, concentrate on your heartbeat. Taking time each day to focus on your breathing can have very soothing and long-lasting effects.

→ As you sit in your garden, what sounds do you hear? Which sounds are from nature and which are man-made?

→ Can you smell what is blooming in your garden? How far from a bloom can you smell it?

* MATERIALS *

- → 1 piece of vinyl or wood lattice, 4' x 8' (122 x 244 cm), cut in half so it's 4' (122 cm) square

- → Paint for wood or vinyl (whichever type of lattice you choose)

- → 3 wooden pallets

- → Exterior paint in several different colors

- → 4 corner braces with screws

- → 2 ½" x 2" x 51" (1.25 x 5.1 x 129.5 cm) pieces of wood for bracing (if necessary)

- → Drill

- → Hammer

- → Screwdriver

- → Finishing nails

- → 3 sticks or dowels or pieces of bamboo, ½" (1.25 cm) diameter, approximately 2' (61 cm) long

- → 3 pieces of fabric at least 2' (61 cm) long and 8" (20 cm) wide

- → Pinking shears

- → Instant fabric and leather adhesive

- → Tension curtain rod

- → 1 pair of curtains, 42" x 36" (106.7 x 91.4 cm)

Forts are the best. Who doesn't need a place to hide once in a while? To start, attach the three pallets to each other as you did when building the compost bin in Lab 26. Do this on level ground and use the four corner braces and screws. Paint the outside of the pallets alternating colors of blue and the inside different shades of green. If using vinyl lattice, attach the wood pieces for bracing along the top front and back of the fort with screws to prevent the lattice roof from sagging.

Fig. 1: Paint the lattice roof and attach it to the fort.

Paint alternating stripes of color on the lattice for the roof and attach it to the pallets using the hammer and finishing nails. (Fig. 1)

Use pinking shears to cut long, tapered triangles for flags from the fabric. You can eyeball it or sketch onto the back of the fabric as a guide. Make the flags at least 20" (51 cm) long. (Fig. 2)

Wrap the wider end of each flag around an end of each bamboo piece. Trim any fabric that sticks out. Apply adhesive to attach the fabric to the bamboo. As this dries, drill guide holes 2" (5 cm) at the other end of the bamboo for attaching them to the pallets. (Fig. 3)

Use the hammer and nails to affix the flagpoles to the back top of the fort. (Fig. 4)

Thread the curtain rod through the curtains and insert the curtain rod into the front opening of the fort. This will run across the front entrance of the fort for privacy. (Fig. 5)

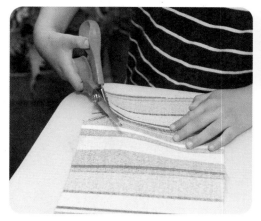

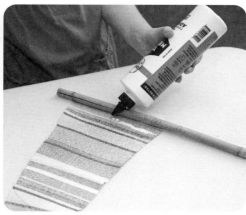

Fig. 2: Cut long, tapered triangle flags.

Fig. 3: Attach the flags and drill guide holes.

Fig. 4: Attach the flagpoles to the fort.

Fig. 5: Position the curtain rod and hang the curtain "door."

|||||||||||||||||||||||||||||||||||||||||||||||||| ✳ **DIG DEEPER!** ✳ ||||||||||||||||||||||||||||||||||||||||||||||

→ Decorate your fort! Use the cushions from Lab 44, use the luminaries from Lab 35 (use battery operated lights in them), get yourself nap-ready with the herb sachets from Lab 46, or sit in your new fort to write in your journal from Lab 42.

* MATERIALS *

→ Fresh herbs from your garden: lavender, chamomile, lemon balm, rose petals

→ Twine

→ Paperclips

→ 6 pieces fabric 8" (20 cm) square

Having trouble sleeping? These selected herbs have calming properties that help lots of people fall asleep. After making this sachet, put it under your pillow or carry it with you during stressful times.

* DIG IN! *

1. Mid to late summer is the best time to harvest your herbs for drying. Collect them in the morning and shake off any water, soil, or bug hitchhikers. (Fig. 1)

2. Tie small bundles of fresh herbs together with the twine and unbend a paperclip to hang them upside down to dry. Keep them away from direct light and check on them in about a week. If the leaves fall away easily from the stems, they are dry and ready to go! (Fig. 2)

3. Once dry, place the herbs, fabric, and twine in your workspace. Take a few leaves and flowers from each type of herb and place in the middle of the fabric. (Fig. 3)

4. Gather up the four corners of the fabric and tie tightly with the twine. Add a sprig of the lavender to the twine for a lovely decorative touch. Your sachet is ready for you to use or give as a gift! (Fig. 4)

Fig. 1: Harvest your herbs.

Fig. 2: Dry your herbs upside down.

Fig. 3: Prepare your workspace.

Fig. 4: Tie the sachet closed.

✳ DIG DEEPER! ✳
KEEP YOUR SACHET SMELLING SWEET

→ When your sachet loses some of its aroma, gently roll it between your hands to crush the leaves and petals to release more scent.

→ Essential oils are extracts from certain plants that have distinct smells and may have medicinal, cleaning, or culinary qualities. It is the essential oils of the herbs used in this activity that cause them to continue giving off their scent for a long time. You can purchase essential oils at natural food stores and add a drop or two to your sachets once their scent has dissipated.

→ Way back in the day, people used sachets to deodorize rooms and themselves. Sachets would be placed either in a closet or room, or hung around the neck like a necklace.

* MATERIALS *

→ Plant specimens

→ 2 wood pieces, 1' (30 cm) square

→ 6 to 10 pieces of corrugated cardboard, slightly smaller than 1' (30 cm) square

→ Newspaper

→ 2 webbing belts (also called utility straps)

Many people are attracted to certain plants because of their flowers. People go crazy over orchid flowers or roses. I'm a sucker for leaves. Coleus, hosta, maple, and spider plant leaves will stop me in my tracks. So many different shapes and sizes and colors, oh my! I can't get enough of them. This is where pressing leaves comes in handy. You can gather leaves any time of year, press them, and use them to display or as a part of gifts. And of course, you can press flowers too!

Fig. 1: Collect your plant specimens.

 * DIG IN! *

1. Collect your plant parts for pressing. Leaves and flowers that are very thick might not press well, but why not experiment anyway? (Fig. 1)

2. Once you are ready to press your specimens, lay one piece of cardboard on top of one piece of wood, followed by two sheets of newspaper. (Fig. 2)

3. Carefully place one leaf or flower on top of the newspaper, then lay two more sheets of paper on top. Repeat the cardboard and newspaper layers (one piece of cardboard, two sheets of newspaper, one plant specimen, two more sheets of newspaper) until you use your last piece of cardboard. Place the second piece of wood on top. (Fig. 3)

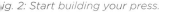

Fig. 2: Start building your press.

Fig. 3: Sandwich your plant samples between newspaper and cardboard.

Fig. 4: Tighten the webbing belts.

4. Wrap the webbing belts around the whole thing and pull the belts tight. Place your plant press in a dry place. It will take several days to absorb the moisture out of the specimens and flatten them out. After about a week, undo the belts and gently lift the newspapers away from your leaves. They are ready to display or use in crafts (see Lab 51). (Fig. 4)

✳ DIG DEEPER! ✳
CREATE AN HERBARIUM SHEET

→ You can use your preserved specimens for crafts or to display or for any number of things. You could also create herbarium sheets: Mount the specimen on paper and write all of the information about the plant, including date and time of collection. Natural history museums and other research institutions make and keep herbarium sheets as a way to document changes in plant populations. For example, they can go back 100 years and look up an herbarium sheet on a plant to see its original range, or region it could be found in, and compare that with the current day. This gives researchers information on climate change, plant diseases, and so on.

* MATERIALS *

→ 1 pair knee-high nylons

→ Wide-mouth drinking glass

→ Spoon

→ Grass seed

→ Soil

→ Googly eyes

→ Waterproof glue, such as Gorilla Glue

→ Felt or foam pieces in various colors

→ Paint pens

→ Small clay pots

→ Small bowl

→ Small plastic or Styrofoam cups, such as Dixie cups

Tip: This is a messy activity, so do this outside if you can. Otherwise spread newspaper on your work surface.

Fill your garden with gnomes to help watch over it and keep you company.
Your garden gnome will be extra special as it will have actual growing "hair"!

 * DIG IN! *

1. Stretch one nylon stocking over the mouth of a wide drinking glass to make pouring the grass seed and soil into the nylon easy. Use a spoon to sprinkle a small handful of grass seed into the stocking. (Fig. 1)

2. Pour one to two handfuls of soil on top of the grass seed, pushing the soil all the way down to the toe. Take the nylon off of the drinking glass, and knot the nylon close to the soil to keep the soil in place. This is your gnome's head. (Fig. 2)

3. With the length of leftover nylon hanging downward, glue googly eyes onto the face area and add other facial features using the felt or foam pieces. Let the glue dry completely. Use the paint pens to paint the clay pots. (Fig. 3)

Fig. 1: Cover the mouth of a drinking glass.

Fig. 2: Pour soil on top of the grass seed, then knot the nylon stocking.

Fig. 3: Glue facial features on the gnome.

Fig. 4: Invert the gnome's head into the water.

Fig. 5: Insert the nylon "wick" into the cup.

4. Fill the bowl with water and invert the gnome's head into it for several minutes. This wets the soil and grass seed and gets the seed growing. (Fig. 4)

5. Insert a small paper cup into a clay pot and fill the cup with water. Flip the gnome's head right side up and insert the loose end of the nylon into the cup. The nylon will act as a wick to pull water up and keep the grass seed watered. Place the gnome where it will get sunlight, and within a week watch for the seed "hair" to sprout! (Fig. 5)

‖‖‖‖‖ * DIG DEEPER! * ‖‖‖‖‖
GRASS FACTS

→ Up to 90 percent of the weight of a grass plant is in its roots.

→ Grass stems are mostly hollow.

→ Grasses are classified as flowering plants.

→ Grassland biomes are found all over the world.

FLOWER ARRANGEMENT

* MATERIALS *

→ Empty spaghetti sauce jar, label removed

→ Pruners

→ Bunch of small sticks that are fairly straight

→ Waterproof silicone adhesive

→ Twine

→ Sharp scissors

→ Flowers from your garden or permission to harvest someone else's

Who doesn't like to get flowers? And giving them is just as fun—especially when the flowers are gifts from your very own garden. Before starting, wash the sauce jar well and remove the label. You may need to soak it in hot, soapy water to remove the label glue.

* DIG IN! *

1. Using the pruners, cut the sticks to the height of the glass jar. Apply a bead of silicone to the outside of the jar and press a stick into it. Continue around the entire jar, creating a fence look, and let it dry for a few hours or overnight. (Fig. 1)

2. Cut two 20" (51 cm) pieces of twine to wrap around and tie at the top and bottom of the jar. This will help hold the sticks in place. (Fig. 2)

3. When you are ready to harvest your flowers, carefully fill your jar halfway with clean, lukewarm water. Avoid getting the glued sticks wet. Collect your flowers first thing in the morning if possible so that they last longer. Cut the stems at a 45° angle. This opens up the most surface area for the stem to take up water. (Fig. 3) Arrange the tallest flowers in the middle of the jar, with shorter flowers around them. Use some leaves around the outer edge for a nice border, and voila! You have a beautiful, handmade creation for someone special (or yourself)!

Fig. 1: Glue the twigs around the jar.

Fig. 2: Tie twine around the jar.

Fig. 3: Cut flower stems at an angle.

* DIG DEEPER! *

WHAT DO YOUR FLOWERS SAY TO YOU?

→ Did you know that flowers have different meanings? Long ago in Victorian times, people would sometimes communicate their feelings through the flowers they sent someone. It was like a code to figure out what a bouquet of different flowers meant! Depending on the source you use, flowers can mean all sorts of different things. Here is just a sampling—read *The Language of Flowers* for more!

Daisy: Innocence
Red rose: Love
Yellow rose: Friendship
Rosemary: Remembrance
Violet: Modesty, loyalty, devotion
Zinnia: Thoughts of friends

* DIG EVEN DEEPER! *

PRESERVING FLOWERS

→ Experiment to see what can be added to the water to preserve cut flowers the longest. Line up a bunch of clean jars and add the same amount of water and same kinds of flower to each. Add lemon juice to one, sugar to one, bleach to one, and so on, and see which keeps your flowers fresh the longest. Make note of this in your garden journal (Lab 42) and tell all your friends!

* MATERIALS *

→ Disposable jar lids of various sizes

→ Magnets

→ Waterproof silicone

→ Small flowers, leaves, and other natural materials that fit into the lids

→ Epoxy resin

→ Disposable jar or cup to mix the epoxy

Tip: Only adults should use the epoxy resin, and it must be used in an area with good ventilation. Wear gloves and cover the work surface with newspapers. Eye protection is also recommended. Doing this activity outside on a clear, warm day would be ideal.

Collect natural materials from your garden that will fit inside the lids, or that can be cut down to size. The items should be fairly flat so they aren't projecting out of the lid.

* DIG IN! *

1. Carefully glue a magnet onto the back of each lid using the silicone. Follow the directions and precautions on the silicone label. Let dry. (Fig. 1)

2. Once the silicone has dried, decide what materials will be in each lid by playing around with different arrangements of leaves, flowers, and other materials together in different lids. Make sure you are happy with the compositions before moving on to the next step. (Fig. 2)

3. An adult should follow the epoxy resin directions for use. Pour the epoxy very slowly over the materials in each lid so the materials don't move around. If they do, use a toothpick to rearrange them. Fill the lids to their rims. (Fig. 3)

Fig. 1: Glue a magnet to each lid.

Fig. 2: Arrange the materials inside the lids.

Fig. 3: Slowly pour the epoxy over the materials.

Fig. 4: Allow the epoxy to dry overnight.

4. Follow the epoxy directions on how to deal with bubbles that appear in your lids after pouring and allow the magnets to dry overnight in a dust-free location. (Fig. 4)

||||||||||||||||||||||||||||||||||| * DIG DEEPER! * |||||||||||||||||||||||||||||||||||||||||||||

TIPS FOR YOUR MAGNET CREATIONS

→ This is another great upcycling activity in which you are keeping items out of the landfill and instead making cool pieces of art that make great gifts. You can use plastic or metal lids. By using smaller, lighter lids you don't need to buy the expensive, heavy-duty magnets.

→ Keep collecting lids so you can do this activity at different times of year. You'll be able to collect different flowers, seeds, and berries from your garden.

* MATERIALS *

→ Fresh leaves in different sizes and colors

→ Plant press (Lab 47)

→ Brown craft paper bag with handles

→ Craft glue

Use the plant press (Lab 47) to flatten and preserve your leaves. They should be ready in one week.

1. Arrange the leaves to your liking on the bag before gluing. (Fig. 1)

2. Carefully lift each leaf up and apply glue to the bag. Press the leaf back down into the glue. Continue gluing all the leaves to the bag. (Fig. 2)

3. Fill the bag with gifts for your favorite person and give it to them on their special day!

Fig. 1: Arrange the leaves on the bag before gluing.

Fig. 2: Glue the leaves onto the bag.

* DIG DEEPER! *
GIVING IS GOOD!

→ Giving gifts to your pals helps strengthen the friendship you have with them.

→ Giving someone a gift usually has very positive effects, especially for the giver!

* MATERIALS *

→ Heavy paper, such as cardstock or construction paper

→ Scissors

→ Pencil

→ Craft glue

→ Various old seeds

This is a creative way to personalize a note to someone special and a great way to use old seeds that aren't viable anymore.

* DIG IN! *

1. Fold or cut the piece of paper into the size you want. Write a message inside the card. Lightly sketch a design or image on the front of the notecard with the pencil. Be as simple or elaborate as you like. (Fig. 1)

Fig. 1: Personalize and design the card.

Fig. 2: Outline your sketch, then cover it with seed.

Fig. 3: Add glue and seeds to one part of the card at a time.

2. Trace over one element of the pencil sketch with the glue. Sprinkle the seeds on top of the glue, completely covering it. (Fig. 2)

3. Continue this process for all of the parts of your card. If you are using different types of seeds for the different images you drew, apply the glue and seeds to one part of the notecard at a time. Set the card aside to dry overnight. Then give it to someone and be prepared to become their best friend. It's true. (Fig. 3)

✷ DIG DEEPER! ✷

OH, SAY CAN YOU SEED?

→ There are two types of seed plants, gymnosperms and angiosperms. Gymnosperm means "naked seed" and includes pines, firs, spruces, and gingkoes. Angiosperm means "seed vessel" and encloses its seeds in a fruit.

→ The largest seed comes from a palm tree and can weigh more than 40 pounds (64 kg)!

→ The smallest seed in the world comes from a tropical orchid; the seeds are so small you can't see them with the naked eye.

* RESOURCES *

Gardening Information

Heat zones in the United States:
American Horticultural Society
www.ahs.org

Outside the United States, find your hardiness zone here:
www.backyardgardener.com/zone/#outside

Order trees and get tons of useful information:
Arbor Day Foundation
www.arborday.org

List of plants that can be toxic to dogs and cats:
The American Society for the Prevention of Cruelty to Animals
www.aspca.org

Tips on planting, insects, and gardening:
Ohio State Extension
www.ohioline.osu.edu

✳ RESOURCES ✳

Tools and Supplies

Garden trowel:
Radius Garden
www.radiusgarden.com

Diverter kit for rain barrels:
Garden Water Saver
http://gardenwatersaver.com

My favorite place to order seeds:
Johnny's Selected Seeds
www.johnnyseeds.com

My favorite place to order perennials:
Bluestone Perennials
www.bluestoneperennials.com

Miniatures and craft items:
Pat Catan's Craft Centers
www.patcatans.com

Josie

Isaac

Jeffrey

Andy

Alex

Nicholas

Joshua

Anna

Alexander

Jordan

Maddie

Lily

Harper

Eva

Isabel

Annabelle

Nate

Thank you to all our gardening lab kids!

* ABOUT THE AUTHOR *

As the Vice President of Education, Renata Fossen Brown oversees the thousands of school children visiting Cleveland Botanical Garden yearly, the development and implementation of teacher professional development workshops, the library, Hershey Children's Garden, and the garden's urban youth farming program, Green Corps. She assisted in the planning and facilitating of a ten-day teacher workshop in Costa Rica to study biodiversity. Brown is involved in the writing of interpretation and exhibit graphics at the garden and served as president of the Cleveland Regional Council of Science Teachers.

Brown holds a B.A. in biology from the University of Toledo and an M.A. in curriculum and instruction from Bradley University, in Peoria, Ill. She is certified to teach grades seven through twelve science, and has been active in informal science education since 1993.

As Assistant Curator of Education at the Toledo Zoo, Brown was responsible for all educational programs occurring on zoo grounds, as well as researching and writing for the zoo's Emmy award-winning television show, *Zoo Today*. Creating and implementing its very first Earth Day celebration is a task of which she is particularly proud. She continued her education role, while adding volunteer coordinator duties and working at Luthy Botanical Garden in Peoria.

A native Clevelander, Renata Fossen Brown gladly returned home in 2004 after a fifteen-year absence. She was named the garden's Clara DeMallie Sherwin Chair in Education in December 2004. She is usually surrounded in her yard by her three dogs and prefers natives and perennials over annuals any day. She is particularly in love with purple coneflower.

www.cbgarden.org

* ACKNOWLEDGMENTS *

Most importantly, thank you to all of my friends and neighbors who let me borrow their children for the creation of this book. Every single one of them amazed me and cracked me up.

To the staff of Cleveland Botanical Garden for giving advice, answering questions, and allowing me the opportunity to write this book, I thank you. Natalie, Ann, Larry, Kathryn, and Geri: Thank you for your support and wisdom.

Many thanks to the Cuyahoga County Soil and Water Conservation District for the hundreds of rain barrels they get out into the community each year and their help with Lab 25!

To the ladies of the Western Reserve Herb Society—you're fantastic and you gave me great ideas, along with a chuckle or two.

To Mary Ann Hall at Quarry Books—thank you for looking me up and giving me such a great opportunity. Your personality made this whole process quite wonderful.

Finally to my husband Dave, who named tools and equipment and gadgets for me, bounced ideas around, walked the dogs when I needed to work, and took absolutely fantastic pictures. Thank you for your patience and support.